# TUCKER TRAILS

## FRANCIS TUCKER
## (The Elder)
## and
## Descendants

First Edition

Edited By
Royal S. Tucker

Based On Unpublished Research
Compiled
by
B. DeRoy Beale

ISBN: 978-0-9968423-5-8



Library of Congress Control Number: 2017930225



Published By:
Royal S. Tucker, LLC
Richmond, Virginia
United States of America

# TABLE OF CONTENTS

# PREFACE

Shortly after publishing "Tucker Trails through Southside Virginia" [1] Reprint Edition, abbreviated here as TTTSV, I learned that original chapters documenting the Francis Tucker family line, intended for the book but not included, were still in existence.

The TTTSV omission is discussed on page 11, as follows: *"This compiler researched the Francis Tucker line primarily to distinguish between the several John Tuckers in both family lines. Research material on the Francis Tucker family line is not included in this book, so that it can be kept within a reasonable number of pages."*

A few Tucker researchers were provided with these unpublished chapters by Mr. Beale. One of those researchers kindly provided them for this book because he felt they should be available to other Tucker researchers.

The sole heir of B. DeRoy Beale has approved, in writing, the publishing, for the first time, of these additional original book chapters.

In preparing this book, the pages have been reformatted to generally replicate the original book. They were received in PDF format digital text files. Very few editing changes have been made in the original content. Changes in the presentation of the information have been made. The Times New Roman font replaces the original typewriter style font. The presentation of tabular content has generally been changed; typically using tables made by the editing program. LibreOffice is an open source software editing program with many capabilities, and it has been the editing program of choice for this book.

The following chapters have been included from TTTSV: REPETITIVE ABBREVIATIONS USED, EARLY TUCKERS, EARLY COUNTIES, CHARLES CITY COUNTY TUCKERS, and PRINCE GEORGE COUNTY TUCKERS.

The numerous original record citations in the book paraphrase and replicate those original documents, including their spelling and punctuation; spelling or punctuation updates for these citations have generally not been added.

In the PREFACE of TTTSV, Mr. Beale expressed his special appreciation to several people for their contributions. One is: "*To my commercial artist friend, Frederick M. Powell, who designed the book cover depicting the trails through Virginia revealed in the Tucker Family Tree.*" The cover art has been used again for this book, with a new title. Special appreciation to Mr. Powell is again expressed by the Editor.

The <u>TABLE of CONTENTS</u> and the <u>INDEX</u> were produced by the editing software.

1. Tucker, Royal S., "Tucker Trails through Southside Virginia", Reprint Edition, 2015; available from <u>Amazon.com</u>.

# CHAPTER CODING

The chapter coding pattern for the partially formatted TTTSV Francis Tucker Line chapters, that are the primary content of this book, is essentially the same as described below for TTTSV.

The only difference being the space after the first letter "T" has a "0" *[zero]* instead of a letter; probably because editing was not complete when the chapters were removed from TTTSV.

The original chapter coding has been retained.

TTTSV CODING

From page 22, near the end of the <u>PRINCE GEORGE COUNTY TUCKERS</u> chapter:

"The coding pattern for the family chapters consists of two parts:

The first four characters identify the family line of one of the sons of Capt Robert Tucker Sr. (who is TR10), from whom all others are descended. (e.g. TG13 = the family line of George Tucker who is third son of Capt Robert Tucker Sr.)

The remaining numbers represent the successive father-son relationship in that family line. (e.g. TG1361 = the 1st son of the 6th son of the 3rd son of Capt Robert Tucker Sr. Trailing zeros of the 8-digit code are reserved for identification of additional generations, which were not researched beyond 1850, except for some in my own family line."

# REPETITIVE ABBREVIATIONS USED

[From Tucker Trails through Southside Virginia]

a - acres
ac - acres
adj- adjacent
b - born
bo - bounds
b.s. - both sides
bro - brother
c - others
ca - circa
d - died
dau - daughter
e.s. - east side
fr - from
incr - increase
l.s. - left side
m - married
md - married
n.s. - north side
rec - recorded
s.s. - south side
u.s. - upper side

Co. - County
Cr. - Creek
DB - Deed Book
Ex. - Executor
Exor. - Executor
Extrx. - Executrix
G - Grant
Jr., Jun., Junr. - Junior
L - English Pounds
MB - Marriage Book
OB - Order Book
P - Patent
Ri. - River
Rd. - Road
S/ - Signed
Sr., Sen., Senr. - Senior
WB - Will Book
Wit. - Witness
wd - will dated
wf - wife
wp - will probated

# EARLY COUNTIES

[From Tucker Trails through Southside Virginia]

In 1634 the Virginia Colony was divided into 7 shires, which were to be governed as shires in England. The designation of shires was soon discontinued and thereafter the sub-divisions were known as counties. The names of the original shires, later counties, were: James City, Henrico, Charles City, Elizabeth City, Warwick River, Warrosquyoake, Charles River and Accowmack.

From Elizabeth City County were formed the counties of Nansemond, Norfolk and Princess Anne.

From Warrosquyoake County were formed the counties of Isle of Wight and Southampton.

From James City County were formed the counties of Surry and Sussex.

Charles City County, at its creation in 1634, included lands on both sides of the James River, on the south side from Upper Chippokes Creek to Appomattox River, and on the north side from Sandy Point to Turkey Island Creek. Charles City County was divided by an act passed in 1702. That part on the north side of the James retained the name of Charles City County. That part on the south side of the James was named Prince George County. [3]

Prince George County was subdivided to form the counties of Brunswick (1732), Amelia (1735) and Dinwiddie (1752). Brunswick County was subdivided to form the counties of Lunenhurg (1746), and Greenville (1781). Lunenhurg County was subdivided to form the counties of Halifax (1752), Bedford (1754), Charlotte (1765) and Mecklenburg (1765). Amelia County was subdivided to form the counties of Prince Edward (1754) and Nottoway (1789). Halifax County was subdivided to form Pittsylvania in 1767.

The Tucker families were among the early settlers of these Southside Virginia counties. Unfortunately, only a few records remain for Charles City, Prince George and Dinwiddie counties, and some have been destroyed for Nottoway and Prince Edward. Generally, records are well preserved for Amelia, Lunenhurg, Mecklenburg, Halifax and Pittsylvania counties.

3. Bell, Landon Covington, "Old Free State", a history of Lunenhurg County Virginia, William Byrd Press, Inc., Richmond, Va.,, Volume 1, 1927.

# EARLY TUCKERS

[From Tucker Trails through Southside Virginia]

The Land Patent books housed in the Virginia State Library provide a valuable source of information about early settlements. Early Tucker families who patented land in the Southside Virginia counties included Capt William Tucker, Thomas Tucker and Robert Tucker.

## CAPT WILLIAM TUCKER & WIFE FRANCES

P 1-29 20 Sep 1624, Capt William Tucker, Elizabeth City Co, 150 ac, w/i corporation of Elizabeth City west of land of Richard Boulton.

P 1-122, 1 Jun, Capt William Tucker, Elizabeth City Co, 100 ac Back Ri w/i precincts of Elizabeth City.

P 1-231, 14 Jul 1635, Capt William Tucker, (county not shown), 200 ac, n.s. of Westernmost Br of Elizabeth Ri, beg at Allington's Cr.

P 1-410, 9 Feb 1636, William Tucker & others, Charles City Co, 8,000 ac, commonly called "Barckley Hundred".

P 1-864, 6 Jan 1642, William Tucker, Upper Norfolk Co, 250 am, w.s. Southward Br. of Nansemond Ri.

Will of William Tucker, Member of the House of Burgesses from Elizabeth City County 1619-1625 [4], William Tucker of the City of London Esq, now bound for the Kingdom of Ireland. 12 Oct 1642. Proved 17 Feb 1643-44. - names: wife Frances, three children, viz sonne William, sonne Thomas and daughter Mary Tucker, brother Thomas Tucker.

Researchers of Tucker families like to claim descendency from this prominent William Tucker. This compiler makes no claim of any evidence to link any of the other Tucker families in this book with this William Tucker. He is shown here as the first Tucker to patent land in Virginia.

## THOMAS TUCKER

P 9-228, 26 Oct 1699, <u>Thomas Tucker</u>, Norfolk Co, 640 ac, w.s. Southern Br of Elizabeth Ri., n.s. Deep Cr.

> *NOTE: This Thomas Tucker may have been the son of Capt William Tucker, but this compiler has no information to suggest this relationship.*

## ROBERT TUCKER

P 6-242, 22 Apr 1669, <u>Robert Tucker</u>, (location not given) 100 ac. on western br of Elizabeth Ri. adj land of the widdow Jennings & Jno Elliott &c. Transp. 2 persons: Richard Murfee & Nath. Dibble.

P 7-424, 21 Oct 1684, <u>Robert Tucker</u>, Lower Norfolk Co, 50 ac n.e. side of main run of Deep Cr. beg at Old Slough's & young Slough's cor. Trans. of Walter Drove.

P 10-453, 11 Dec 1719, <u>Robert Tucker</u>, Norfolk Co, 81 ac in Norfolk Co, & 3 lots of 1/2 ac in Town of Norfolk. Escheat land formerly belonging to Rosamund Tabor of about 100 ac, upon a survey found to contain but 81 ac.

P 18-99, 12 Sep 1738, <u>Robert Tucker</u>, Norfolk Co, 1 1/2 ac. escheat land near Norfolk Town btwn Edward Portlock & John Munds decd.

P 23-921, 10 Jul 1745, <u>Robert Tucker</u>, Norfolk Co, 3 ac, 60 sq. po., in Borough of Norfolk, adj his lott where he now liveth.

SUMMARY: This William Tucker, b before 1691, m before 1721, Elizabeth ____, & had issue:

> Susanna Tucker b 19 Apr 1721.
> George Tucker b 4 Sep 1723.
> Daniel Tucker b 29 Jan 1725.

## JOSEPH TUCKER

PATENTS [17]

P-10-402, 14 Jul 1718, <u>Joseph Tucker</u> <u>403 ac</u>, Pr Geo Co, b.s. Stony Cr.

P 11-117, 22 Jun 1722, <u>Joseph Tucker</u>, <u>180 ac</u>, Pr Geo Co, head of Reedy Br of Sappone Cr, <u>adj. Geo Tillman</u>, Harry's Swamp.

*NOTE: Notice also that Robert Tucker owned land in 1719 adj. John Tillman, on Monks Neck Cr.*

P 13-462, 28 Sep 1730, <u>Joseph Tucker</u> <u>150 ac</u>, Pr Geo Co, s.s. Stony Cr, adj his old land.

P 14-23, 28 Sep 1730, <u>Joseph Tucker</u>, <u>302 ac</u>, Pr Geo Co, l.s. Beaverpond Cr, <u>adj Robt Wynn</u>. *(Note: See comment below.)*

P 18-679, 10 Jun 1740, <u>Joseph Tucker</u>, <u>739 ac</u>, Pr Geo Co, l.s. Beaverpond .Br, ____ Ri, adj & including his old (?line).

P 19-687, 10 Jun 1740, <u>Joseph Tucker</u>, <u>400 ac</u>, Pr Geo Co, l.s. Reedy Br of Stony Cr.

P 26-426, 5 Apr 1748, <u>Joseph Tucker</u>, <u>138 ac</u>, Pr Geo Co, head of Mirey Br of Beaverpond Cr, adj Peter Thomas & Jackson's lines.

P 31-622, 10 Sep 1755, <u>Joseph Tucker</u> & Stephen Evans, Dinwiddie Co, <u>430 ac</u>, n.s. Sapone Cr.

P 22-457, 20 Aug 1745, <u>Joseph Tucker Jr</u>, <u>286 ac</u>, Pr Geo Co, u.s. Plat Br of Stony Cr.

*NOTE: If Joseph Tucker Jr was at least age 21 when he patented land in 1745, then he was b before 1724.*

P 22-538, 20 Sep 1745, <u>Joseph Tucker Jr</u>, <u>400 ac</u>, Pr Geo Co, btn Stony & Sappone Cr, adj Richd Harrison, <u>Joseph Tucker</u> & c.

P 33-232, 16 Aug 1756, <u>Joseph Tucker Jr</u>, <u>46 ac</u>, Pr Geo Co, n.s. Stony Cr, adj Melone, Wingfield

PRINCE GEORGE CO, VA. [18]

p 16, 17 Jun 1714, rec 13 Jul 1714. Indenture btwn John Coleman & Robert Munford, for 10 ac in Bristol Parish, Pr Geo Co, next to Coleman & Munford on the river, for 1400 lbs tobacco & 10 shillings. <u>Wit</u>: Charles Roberts, <u>Joseph Tucker</u>

p 750, Survey, 19 Hay 1712, <u>Joseph Tucker</u>, <u>100 ac</u>, w.s. Numisseen Cr, adj above survey (of William Coleman Sr.)

*NOTE: If Joseph Tucker was at least age 21 when he surveyed land in 1712, then he was b before 1691. However, no patent was found for this 100 ac. p 752, Survey, 20 Oct 1715, <u>Joseph Tucker, 403 ac</u>, b.s. Stony Cr. (See Patent 10-402.)*

*NOTE: The above Robert Tucker is probably not the same Robert Tucker who patented land in Charles City Co in 1680. No relation is determined or implied by this compiler. See next chapter.*

Under the headright system, many other colonists were imported, and the person paying the transportation cost was granted 50 acres of land for each person imported (known as a headright). Other Tuckers, who came to the southern counties of the colony as headrights, included the following: [5]

| | | |
|---|---|---|
| 1635 | Alex. Tucker | Warrasquioake Co. |
| 1638 | Allen Tucker | Charles City Co. |
| 1639 | Barthol. Tucker | Upper Norfolk Co. |
| 1649 | Alice Tucker | James City Co. |
| 1650 | William Tucker | Charles City Co. |
| 1666 | William Tucker | Isle of Wight Co. |
| 1673 | Eliz. Tucker | Isle of Wight Co. |
| 1680 | John Tucker | Charles City Co. |
| 1683 | John Tucker | Charles City Co. |
| 1688 | Samll Tucker | Lower Norfolk Co. |
| 1688 | Tho. Tucker | Isle of Wight Co. |

These colonists may or may not have settled in the same area as the person who paid their transportation, and they were not further researched by this compiler.

\* \* \*

4. Virginia Historical Magazine, Vol. 22, pg 267.
5. Nugent, Nell Marion, "Cavaliers and Pioneers", Vol I, 1934, Vol II, 1937.

# CHARLES CITY COUNTY TUCKERS

[From Tucker Trails through Southside Virginia]

## ROBERT TUCKER & WIFE ELIZABETH

*NOTE: A close but undefined relationship existed between Robert and Francis Tucker and the Coleman families.*

PATENTS [6]

P 5-166, 18 Mar 1662. <u>John Coleman</u>, Chas. City Co, 813 ac, s.s. Appomattox Ri adj Mr. Tounstall.

P 5-519, 20 Oct 1665, <u>Robert Coleman Jr.</u>, Chas. City Co, 450 ac, s.s. Appomatox Ri, beg at Robert Coleman Sr's head line.

P 6-181, 25 Sep 1667, <u>Robert Coleman</u>, Isle of Wight Co, 634 ac, beg Cyprus Br.

P 6-189, 29 Oct 1668, <u>Robert Coleman Sr</u>, Chas. City Co, 283 ac, s.s. Appamattox Ri, btwn Henry Leadbeater & sd Coleman, thence to head line of the Island patent.

P 8-422, 21 Apr 1695, <u>Robert Coleman</u>, Isle of Wight Co, 80 ac, in lower marsh adj Thomas Jordan & Giles Driver.

P 9-109, 28 Oct 1697, <u>Robert Coleman</u>, Nansemond Co, 450 ac. near Wickham swamp, adj Thomas & John Milner.

P 7-29, 20 Apr 1680, <u>Robert Tucker</u>, Charles City Co, 172 ac, n.s. Blackwater, adj Wm. Jones, Jordan's path, Edward Bircherd, the Reedy Br, Baynes' path & c. <u>Transp 4 persons. Jno Tucker, 3 times,</u> Sar. Twill.

*NOTE: If Robert Tucker was at least age 21 when he patented land in 1680, then he was b before 1659.*

Patent (Nugent p 303), 30 Oct 1686, Mr. Edward Birchett, Chas. City Co., 230 ac. in Bristol Parish on n.s. Main Blackwater, <u>adj. Mr. Robert Tucker</u>. Transp 5 persons.

*NOTE: The above land became Prince George Co. in 1703.*

p 180, 18 Dec 1688. <u>John, orphan of Robert Coleman</u>, chooses his brother <u>Robert Coleman</u>, his guardian.

*NOTE: Robert Coleman (Sr.) d 1688, leaving son Robert Coleman (Jr.) & minor son John Coleman.*

p 180, 18 Dec 1688. <u>Robert Coleman</u> granted administration of <u>Warner Coleman's</u> estate.

*NOTE: Warner Coleman d 1688. Was he also a son of Robert Coleman Sr?*

p 181, 18 Dec 1688. If witnesses to <u>Robert Coleman</u>'s will do not appear at next court to prove same, they will be fined.

p 202, 3 Apr 1689, Administration granted Hon. Wm. Byrd, Esq, on est of <u>Jno. Coleman decd</u>, the widow assenting. Mr. Jno Mays, Ja. Hall & Edward Birchett to inventory est. Capt. Hen. Batte & Mr. Robert Bolling to swear them.

*NOTE: John Coleman d 1689. Was he a brother of Robert Coleman Sr? Notice the name Edward Birchett, who owned land adj to Robert Tucker on n.s. the Blackwater (Patent 7-29)*

p 242, 16 Sep 1689. Administration granted <u>Fra. Tucker</u> on estate of <u>Warner Coleman</u>, dec'd; and Jarvis Dix and <u>Francis Coleman</u> give bond.

*NOTE: Francis Tucker replaced Robert Coleman (Jr) as admr of Warner Coleman. Was Francis Tucker a son-in-law of Robert Coleman Sr? Was Francis Coleman also a son of Robert Coleman Sr?*

p 242, 16 Sep 1689. Ordered that estate of <u>Warner and John Coleman, dec'd</u> be delivered to <u>Francis Tucker, Adm'r., of Warner Coleman</u>. <u>Robert Coleman</u>, who is possessed with those estates, submits to this order in court.

p 242, 16 Sep 1689. Estate of <u>Robert Coleman</u> in hands of <u>Robert Tucker</u> to be inventoried and Capt. Henry Batte to assign and swear appraisers and take secuity for delivery of legacies.

*NOTE: Was Robert Tucker a son-in-law of Robert Coleman Sr?*

p 426, 3 Oct 1692. Judgement granted <u>Robert Tucker agst Francis Tucker</u> for 1717 lbs tobacco.

P - 482, 1693. Persons assigned court surveyors of the highways - included Mr James Thewat & Mr. <u>Robert Tucker</u> for Apamatox.

p 555, 4 Feb 1694. Deed of land by <u>Robert Coleman</u> and <u>Robert Tucker and Elizabeth his wife</u>, by her attorney Richard Bland, to Francis Hobson is proved by John Heath and Solomon Crook.

*NOTE: Was Elizabeth Tucker a dau of Robert Coleman Sr? And did Robert Coleman (Jr) & Robert Tucker (in right of his wife Elizabeth) sell land inherited from Robert Coleman Sr?*

p 555, 4 Feb 1694. Lease of 50 acres of land by Abraham Coulston to Daniel Sandburne ano 1675 and a lease of same 50 acres by said Sandburne to <u>Robert Tucker</u> ano 1676 and both endorsed with assignment of <u>Robert Tucker and Elizabeth his wife</u> to John Butler, and acknowledged by Tucker and his wife by Richard Bland her attorney, and recorded.

*NOTE: The above item is most confusing, in that the transactions which occurred in 1675-76 were not recorded until 18 years later in 1694. If the dates are correct, then that Robert Tucker would have been born before 1655, and would have married Elizabeth before 1675. (See Patent 7-29, 1680).*

*NOTE: While there is no direct evidence, this compiler believes the records above suggest that Robert Tucker's wife Elizabeth, and Francis Tucker's wife (later identified as Mary) were each a Coleman. There are no salvaged records for Charles City Co. and Prince George Co for the period 1695-1712. No will was found for Robert Tucker, but he may have died before 1704, for Elizabeth Tucker held 212 ac in the Prince George Quit Rents of 1704.* [8]

## JOHN TUCKER

### CHARLES CITY CO, VA [9]

*NOTE: Notice in Robert Tucker's Patent 7-29, 1680, cited above, that Robert Tucker transported John Tucker three times. No patents were found for this John Tucker.*

p 571, 3 Jun 1695. John Tucker of Martins Brandon Parish, exhibits a certificate from the vestry of his inability to labor and is discharged from parish levy and is discharged from county and public levy's.

### PRINCE GEORGE CO, VA. 1713-1728 [10]

p 133, 18 Aug 1716, rec 13 Nov 1716, will of John Tucker of Martins Brandon Parish, Pr. Geo. Co., names: widow Ann Jackson, executor, God-dau Elizabeth Jackson, Mary Thornhill, Thomas Daniell, James Cragg, William Smith, widow Blayton. Wit: Thomas Daniel, Eliza. x Jackson.

*NOTE: John Tucker d 1716, apparently without issue.*

### FRANCIS TUCKER

*NOTE: See section on Robert Tucker above for transactions involving both Robert Tucker and Francis Tucker in Charles City Co.*

### PATENTS [11]

P 10-339, 15 Jul 1717, Francis Tucker, Pr Geo Co, 289 ac, b.s. Mawhipponock Cr, adj Herbert's land.

### PRINCE GEORGE CO, VA. 1713-1728 [12]

p 663, 12 Dec 1722, rec 10 Dec 1723, will of Francis Tucker
names: wife Mary;
son Francis - land e.s. Mawhipponoak Cr at lower end;
son John - land on n.s. same cr adj Henry Mayes;
son Henry - land btwn sons Francis & John, incl plantation where I live;
son Abram - land on n.s Mawhipponoak Cr adj son Henry & Thomas Mitchell;

son <u>Mathew</u>, land adj Thomas Mitchell
Wit: Mathew Mayes, Henry Mayes, John Powell.

*NOTE: Francis Tucker did not patent any land in the original Charles City Co. The 289 ac which he patented in Prince George Co. in 1717, and willed to his sons in 1723, lay in the area which became Dinwiddie Co. in 1752.*

*NOTE: Research revealed that the descendants of Francis Tucker perpetuated the given names Francis, John, Henry, Abram & Mathew. This contrasts significantly with the descendants of Robert Tucker who perpetuated the given names Robert, James, George, John, William, Joseph & Daniel. Except for the name John, each family rarely used the given names of the other. They seemed to have become completely separate family lines.*

*This compiler researched the Francis Tucker line primarily to distinguish between the several John Tuckers in both family lines. Research material on the Francis Tucker family line is not included in this book, so that it can be kept within a reasonable number of pages.*

*Apparently the Francis Tucker line has already been researched by others, as evidenced by a group of family charts made available to me.*

*NOTE: Salvaged Prince George Co. records include land surveys and other references for the next generation of Tuckers.*

6. Card File of Land Patents and Grants, Virginia State Library Archives.

7. Weisiger, Benjamin B. III, "Charles City County, Virginia Court Orders 1687-1695", reprinted 1984.

8. Boddie, John B., "Historical Southern Families", Vol 5.

9. Weisiger, Benjamin B. III, "Charles City County, Virginia Court Orders 1687-1695", reprinted 1984.

10. Weisiger, Benjamin B. III, "Prince George County, Virginia Wills & Deeds 1713-1728", 1973.

11. Card File of Land Patents and Grants, Virginia State Library Archives.

12. Weisiger, Benjamin B. III, "Prince George County, Virginia Wills & Deeds 1713-1728", 1973.

# PRINCE GEORGE COUNTY TUCKERS

[From Tucker Trails through Southside Virginia]

As pointed out in a previous chapter, that part of Charles City County which lay south of the James River became Prince George County in 1703. Generally it encompassed the area south of the James and Appomattox Rivers, and in a southwestward direction to the North Carolina border. From Prince George were formed the counties of Brunswick (1732), Amelia (1735) and Dinwiddie (1752).

Most of Prince George County records were destroyed during the civil war. There are no records for this area from 1696-1712. Salvaged Deed and Will Books 1713-1728 and some court records 1733-1792 have been extracted by Weisiger, and are cited throughout this book.

These salvaged records include lists of land surveys made by surveyor Robert Bolling during the period 1710-1725, and many other references to Tucker Families, including Francis, John, Matthew, Robert, William, Joseph, Daniel, and James Tucker.

Research information for Francis Tucker identified his sons John and Matthew *(above)*, and Francis, Henry and Abram. *(See previous chapter.)* The Francis Tucker family is not included in the remainder of this book.

Robert, William, Joseph and Daniel Tucker were probably brothers and may have been sons of the Robert Tucker & wf Elizabeth (? Coleman) of Charles City Co, cited in the previous chapter. See citations following.

## WILLIAM TUCKER

PATENTS [13]

P 10-446, 11 Jul 1719, William Tucker, Pr Geo Co, 143 ac, n.s. Stony Cr.

P 11-337, 20 Feb 1723, William Tucker, Pr Geo Co, 300 ac, b.s. Turkey Egg Cr, n.s. Nottoway Ri.

P 12-508, 7 Jul 1726, <u>William Tucker</u>, Brunswick Co, <u>361 ac</u>, sm br of Cocke Cr, n.s. Roanoke Ri.

P 14-19, 28 Sep 1730, <u>William Tucker</u>, Pr Geo Co, <u>200 ac</u>, l.s. Beaverpond Cr, adj Matthew Sturdivant & Robert Wynne.

PRINCE GEORGE CO, VA. [14]

p 749, Survey, 20 May 1712, <u>William Tucker</u>, 100 ac, w.s. Numosseen Cr.

*NOTE: If this William Tucker was at least age 21 when he surveyed land in 1712, then he was b before 1691. However, no patent was found for this 100 ac.*

p 753, Survey, 20 Oct 1715, <u>William Tucker</u>, <u>143 ac</u>, n.s. Stony Cr. *(See Patent 10-446.)*

p 818, Survey, 1 Feb 1724, <u>William Tucker</u>, <u>200 ac</u>, l.s. Beaver Pond Cr, adj his own land. *(See Patent 14-19.)*

p 745, 13 Oct 1724, <u>William Tucker & wf Elizabeth</u> to William Mallone, son of Nathaniel Mallone of Surry Co, <u>143 ac</u> on n.s. Stony Cr in Pr Geo Co. Wit: George Hamilton Jr, Michael Wallis, Litt. Hardyman. *(See Patent 10-446.)*

*NOTE: Notice that William Tucker's wife was also named Elizabeth.*

p 994, 13 Oct 1726, rec 13 Jun 1727. Francis Bressie of Pr Geo Co to <u>William Tucker of Elizabeth City Co</u>, for L10, 200 ac on Stony Cr, Pr Geo, being part of a tract granted to Francis Bressie by patent in 1726. <u>Bo. by sd Tucker</u>, John Manson, Henry Maynard, Chamberlains Bedd, Stony Cr. Wit: William Tucker, William Bressie, Randolph Snowden, Ellyson Armistead, Thomas Smith.

*NOTE: Could this William Tucker, <u>1726</u> of Elizabeth City Co, be a descendant of the Capt. William Tucker who patented land 100 years earlier, <u>1624-35</u> in Elizabeth City Co? Notice also that another William Tucker witnessed this deed.*

## BRISTOL PARISH VESTRY BOOK [15]

The Bristol Parish Vestry Book includes an entry pertaining to the continuing relationship between the Coleman and Tucker families:

"17 Sep 1721. Upon the petition of Wm. Tucker sheweth that Robt Coleman lys at his house in a very weak helpless condition & has been so these six months past, which grows very changeable & trouhelesome to the sd Tucker. Tis ord that Wm. Tucker take care of the foresd Robt Coleman & find him such necessaries as is convenient and at the next levie, the sd Tucker to bring his account to the vestry & what is thought just to be allowed from the parish. Tis further ordered that the church wardens enquire how the foresd Robt Coleman gave his estate to Robert Tucker Senr & upon what terms."

## BRISTOL PARISH REGISTER [16]

Susanna dau of Wm & Eliz:Tucker born 19th of April 1721 bap 14th feb 1722-3.

Geo S: of Wm & Eliz: Tucker born 4th Septr 1723 bapt 11th octobr 1724.

Daniel Son of William and Eliza Tucker born 29th Janr 1725.

The land which William Tucker surveyed, patented and bought in Pr Geo Co, lay in the area which became Dinwiddie Co in 1752, and no further information on this family was available to this compiler.

*NOTE: Also on p 752, Survey, 20 Oct 1715, Joseph Wynne, 153 ac, b.s. Stony Cr. (See comment below.)*

p 756, Survey, 24 Nov 1719, Joseph Tucker, 180 ac, on head of Reedy Br of Sapponee. *(See Patent 11-117.)*

## BRISTOL PARISH REGISTER [19]

Robt son of Joss: & Martha Tucker born 3d of Octobr Last bapt May 28th 1721.

David Son of Joseph and Martha Tucker Born 24th Dcember 1729

Bapt 31th May 1730.

Lucretia D of <u>Joseph & Lucretia Tucker</u> Born 15th august 1731 Bapt 10th octber.

Mary D. of <u>Joseph & Lucretia Tuckers</u> born Aprile 3d & hapd May 26th 1745.

*NOTE: Boddie [20] states that "Joseph Tucker, son of Robert & Martha, was b about 1710 -- married Lucretia, daughter of Maj Robert Wynne -- , & names children born beginning in 1731 --", This cannot be correct, since Joseph son of Robert & Martha was not born until 22 Jun 1722. (See chapter for Capt Robert Tucker Sr.) The Joseph Tucker who m Lucretia Wynne was most probably the subject Joseph Tucker who was b before 1691, who surveyed land in 1712, & who patented land 1730 <u>adj Robert Wynn</u> (Patent 14-23). Also, Boddie's account of the children of Joseph & Lucretia was inconsistent with the Bristol Parish Register.*

*NOTE: The lands which Joseph Tucker and Joseph Tucker Jr surveyed and patented in Pr Geo Co, lay in the area which became Dinwiddie Co in 1752, and no further information on this family was available to this compiler.*

SUMMARY: Joseph Tucker, b before 1691, m 1st before 1720 Martha ____, m 2nd before 1731 Lucretia ____ & had issue:

Robert Tucker b 3 Oct 1720.
Joseph Tucker Jr b before 1724.
David Tucker b 24 Dec 1729.
Lucretia Tucker b 15 Aug 1731.
Mary Tucker b 3 Apr 1745.

<u>DANIEL TUCKER</u>

PRINCE GEORGE CO, VA. [21]

p 761, Survey, 18 Dec 1722 <u>Daniel Tucker</u>, <u>129 ac</u>, w.s. Reedy Br. Sapponnee. *(See Patent 12-229.)*

*NOTE: If this Daniel Tucker was at least age 21 when he surveyed land in 1722, then he was b before 1701.*

PATENTS [22]

P 12-229, 22 Feb 1724, <u>Daniel Tucker</u>, Pr Geo Co, 129 ac, u.s. Reedy Br btwn <u>his brother Jos. Tucker</u> & Maj Robert Munford.

*NOTE: This is another indication that Daniel and Joseph Tucker were brothers.*

BRISTOL PARISH REGISTER [23]

Nevil Son of <u>Daniel & Eliza Tucker</u> Born 25th aprill 1730.

PRINCE GEORGE CO., VA.[24]

p 384, 12 Feb 1739, Will of <u>Daniel Tucker</u> exhibited in court by <u>Elizabeth Tucker</u> , his relict & executrix. Will was proved by oaths of <u>Joseph Tucker, William Tucker</u>, & Robert Whitehall, witnesses, and probate granted.

*NOTE: The above is further indication that Daniel, Joseph and William Tucker were brothers, and probably sons of the earlier Robert Tucker & wf Elizabeth (?Coleman) of Charles City Co. Furthermore, Capt Robert Tucker Sr. was also probably their brother, because he named his last three sons William, Joseph and Daniel. (See next chapter).*

The land which Daniel Tucker surveyed and patented in Prince George Co lay in the area which became Dinwiddie Co in 1752, and no further information was available to this compiler.

SUMMARY: Daniel Tucker b before 1701, d 1739 Pr Geo Co, m before 1730 Elizabeth ____, & had issue:

Nevil Tucker b 25 Apr 1730.

<u>ROBERT TUCKER</u>

As stated earlier in this chapter, this compiler has a conviction that William Tucker, Joseph Tucker, Daniel Tucker and Robert Tucker of Prince George Co, were probably brothers, and probably sons of an earlier Robert Tucker & wife Elizabeth (?Coleman) of Charles City Co (circa 1676). There is ample evidence that the Tucker and Coleman families migrated together, owned adjacent lands, and participated together in legal matters.

# BRISTOL PARISH VESTRY BOOK [25]

The Bristol Parish Vestry Book includes an entry pertaining to the relationship between the Coleman and Tucker families:

> "17 Sep 1721. Upon the petition of <u>Wm. Tucker</u> sheweth that <u>Robt Coleman</u> lys at his house in a very weak helpless condition & has been so these six months past, which grows very changeable & troubelesome to the sd Tucker. Tis ord that <u>Wm. Tucker</u> take care of the foresd <u>Robt Coleman</u> & find him such necessaries as is convenient and at the laying of the next levie, the sd Tucker to bring his account to the vestry & what is thought just to be allowed from the parish. Tis further ord that the church wardens enquire how the foresd <u>Robt Coleman gave his estate to Robt Tucker Senr</u> & upon what terms."

*NOTE; The above Robert Tucker Sr seems to be the same Capt Robert Tucker Sr who d Amelia Co, 1750, but different from the Robert Tucker named in Charles City Co. Court Order p 242, 16 Sep 1689 (32 years earlier) in which a Robert Coleman's estate was in hands of a Robert Tucker.*

There is evidence that the subject Robert Tucker owned land on s.s. Appomattox Ri in Prince George Co before 1714.

# PRINCE GEORGE CO, VA, [26]

p 43, 7 Feb 1714/15 Deed. Matthew Anderson Jr of Bristol Parish, Pr Geo Co, to Robert Munford of same, 100 ac, <u>next to</u> Math Mayse, John Mayse, "Haycocks", <u>Robert Tucker</u>, Capt John Coleman, & sd Munford, formerly belonging to William Byrd, Esq.

p 44, 8 Feb 1714/15. Mathew Anderson Jr of Bristol Parish, Pr Geo Co, to Robert Munford of same, 100 ac, bo Mathew Mayse, John Mayse, sd Mundford's land "Haycocks", <u>Robert Tinker (Tucker?)</u> & Capt John Coleman, & sd Munford's land which formerly belonged to Wm Byrd, Esq, & John Mayse.

*NOTE: If this Robert Tucker was at least age 21, when he owned land in 1714, then he was b before 1693.*

p 160, 14 May 1717, <u>Robert Tucker</u> of Bristol Parish, Pr Geo Co, to avid Crawley of same, <u>200 ac</u>, bo Appomattox Ri, Maj Robert Bolling, John Coleman, Maj Robert Munford.

*NOTE: Since no patent was found, it can be assumed that Robert Tucker either bought the above 200 ac. or inherited it. See previous chapter for a discussion of an earlier Robert Tucker & wf Elizabeth (circa 1676), and patents of Robert Coleman & John Coleman on s.s. Appomattox Ri in Charles City Co.*

*NOTE: There is evidence also that the subject Robert Tucker owned land in the area of Monks Neck Cr (spelled variously) in Pr Geo Co, and that he was closely associated with the Parham and Tillman families.*

p 364, 12 Oct 1719, rec 13 Oct 1719. <u>John Tillman</u> of Pr Geo Co to Richard Cooke of York Co, 100 ac on <u>n.s. Monksneck Cr</u> on mouth of Russell Br, on <u>Robert Tucker's line</u>.

*NOTE: Since no patent was found for Robert Tucker's land on Monks Neck Cr, it is assumed he either bought or inherited it. It lay in the area of Pr Geo Co which became Dinwiddie Co in 1752. An old map of Dinwiddie Co. in the Archives of Virginia State Library, shows Monks Neck Rd going east from Dinwiddie Courthouse (roughly present county road 605), and crossing Monks Neck Cr, flowing south (now the northernmost part of Rowanty Cr).*

*NOTE: Early patents include: Roger Tilman, Patent 7-107, 20 Apr 1689, Charles City Co, 1,060 ac, s.s. Appomattox Ri, at a place known as <u>Moncus-a-Neak</u>. Also Thomas Parham & Henry King, Patent 8-76, 21 Apr 1690, Charles City Co, 824 ac, at or near <u>Moncosaneak</u>, beg land of <u>late Roger Tyllman</u> on the side of the great branch. Roger Tillman probably was b long before 1668, & d before 1690. Thomas Parham probably was b before 1669.*

p 144, 19 Nov 1716, rec 12 Mar 1716 (?1717). <u>Will of Susannah Tillman</u>, aged 69. To <u>son Thomas Parram</u>, son George Tillman, son John Tillman, dau Jane Robinson, dau Christian Abernathy, grandau Mary Bethell all miscellaneous items. To grandson Robert Abernathy - all remainder of est & to be exor.

*NOTE: Susannah ____ was b ca 1647, m 1st after 1663 (after age 16), ____ Parham, & had issue Thomas Parham, b before 1669. Susannah m 2nd after 1669 Roger Tillman (d ca 1690) & had issue George, John, Jane, & Christian Tillman. George Tillman, who surveyed land Mar 1711, probably was b btwn 1670-1690.*

p 168, 5 Feb 1716, rec 14 May 1717. <u>Will of Thomas Parram</u>. To Nicholas Robyson - 100 ac <u>btwn Monck's Neck & Cattail Run</u>, which did formerly belong to George Tillman, & after to William Hulm. To John Tillman - 50 ac on <u>n.s. Monks Neck Cr</u>. To my son Thomas Parram - several items. To son William Parram - plantation I now live on, 100 ac. To dau Amy Jones - a cow. To <u>dau Eliza.Tucker</u> - cow & steer. To dau Feebe several items. To dau Susannah - cow & calf. To dau Jane - cow & calf. To loving <u>wife Eliza</u> - all remainder of est & to be exec. Wit. Geo. Tillman, Robert Abernathy, John Patteson. Brought in by Elizabeth Parram, exec.

*NOTE: Thomas Parham (b before 1669, d 1716/17) was son of Susannah Parham Tillman (1647-1717) whose first husband was Parham, and whose second husband was Roger Tillman. Thomas Parham's half brothers & sisters were George Tillman, John Tillman, Jane Robinson, and Christian Abernathy. Thomas Parham md Elizabeth ____, and they had issue: Thomas Parham, William Parham, Amy Jones, <u>Elizabeth Tucker</u>, & Feebe, Susannah & Jane Parham. These references suggest also that Thomas Parham's dau Elizabeth Tucker may have been the wife of Robert Tucker who owned land near Tillman and Parham on Monks Neck Creek.*

Boddie [27] suggests that the earlier Robert Tucker d before 1704, was m to Elizabeth Parham dau of Thomas Parham, and they were the parents of Robert Tucker who m Martha, and settled in Amelia Co.

The earlier Robert Tucker, whose wife was Elizabeth as early as

1676, was b probably before 1655. If Elizabeth was at least age 15 when m to Robert Tucker in 1676, she probably was b before 1660, and would have been at least age 56 in 1716 when Thomas Parham died. She would have been older than Thomas Parham, and could not have been his daughter. Thus the earlier Elizabeth Tucker wife of Robert Tucker was not the same Elizabeth Tucker dau of Thomas Parham.

If Thomas Parham was b before 1669, and m before 1690, then his dau Elizabeth was b probably before 1691, & m _____ Tucker before 1707, and would have been at least age 25 in 1716 when her father died. All these dates could be earlier.

If Susannah Tillman was age 69 when she wrote her will in 1716, she was b ca 1647. If Susannah m Parham after age 16 in 1663, then her son Thomas Parham was b after 1663 and before 1669, was m after 1684. Therefore Thomas Parham's dau Elizabeth Tucker was b after 1684, m after 1700, and could not be the same "Elizabeth wf of Robert Tucker" shown in Charles City Co. reference p 555 in 1676-1694.

The subject Robert Tucker was b before 1693 (perhaps as early as 1676), and may have been the son of the earlier Robert Tucker who was b before 1655 & who was m to Elizabeth (?Coleman). Elizabeth Parham may have m the subject Robert Tucker, but she would have been very young, for the subject Robert Tucker is known to have had a son James b ca 1698.

It should be remembered from previous discussions, however, that (1) William Tucker's, wife was also named Elizabeth as early as 1721, and they had a dau named Susannah, and (2) Daniel Tucker's wife was also named Elizabeth, and they had a son as early as 1730. So - did Thomas Parham's dau Elizabeth Tucker marry Robert Tucker, or William Tucker, or Daniel Tucker? The incomplete salvaged records of Prince George Co do not provide the answers.

This compiler suggests that the earlier Robert Tucker (ca 1655-1704) m Elizabeth (?Coleman), and their sons were Robert, William, Joseph & Daniel. Their son the subject Robert Tucker (ca

1676-1750) m 1st ca 1698 Elizabeth Parham (ca 1684-1719), and m 2nd before 1720, Martha ____. I should like to suggest further that this subject Robert Tucker was the same Capt Robert Tucker Sr who d 1750 in Amelia Co, who is the subject of the next chapter, and who was the ancestor of the Tuckers in the remaining chapters of this book.

The coding pattern for the remaining chapters consists of two parts. The first four characters identify the family line of one of the sons of Capt Robert Tucker Sr (who is TR10), from whom all others are descended. (e.g. TG13 = the family line of George Tucker who is third son of Capt Robert Tucker Sr.) The remaining numbers represent the successive father-son relationship in that family line. (e.g. TG1361 = the 1st son of the 6th son of the 3rd son of Capt Robert Tucker Sr. Trailing zeros of the 8-digit code are reserved for identification of additional generations, which were not researched beyond 1850, except for some in my own family line.

This book identifies the descendants of Capt Robert Tucker Sr, from about 1700 to 1850, documented with citations from land patents, deeds, wills, marriages, births, tithables, personal tax, and land tax, as they migrated through the Virginia counties of Charles City, Prince George, Amelia, Nottoway, Prince Edward, Lunenburg, Mecklenburg, Halifax and Pittsylvania.

* * *

13. Card File of Land Patents and Grants, Virginia State Library Archives.

14 Weisiger, Benjamin B., III, "Prince George County, Virginia, Wills & Deeds 1713-1728", 1973.

15. Bristol Parish Vestry Book, Virginia State Library.

16. Boddie, John B., "Births 1720-1792 from the Bristol Parish Register of Henrico, Prince George and Dinwiddie".

17. Card File of Land Patents and Grants, Virginia State Library Archives.

18. Weisiger, Benjamin B., III, "Prince George County, Virginia, Wills & Deeds 1713-1728", 1973.

19. Boddie, John B., "Births 1720-1792 from the Bristol Parish Register of Henrico, Prince George and Dinwiddie".

20. Boddie, John B., "Historical Southern Families", Vol 5, p 296.

21. Weisiger, Benjamin B., III, "Prince George County, Virginia, Wills & Deeds 1713-1728", 1973.

22. Card File of Land Patents and Grants, Virginia State Library Archives.

23. Boddie, John B., "Births 1720-1792 from the Bristol Parish Register of Henrico, Prince George and Dinwiddie".

24. Weisiger, Benjamin B., III, "Prince George County, Virginia Records 1733-1792", 1975.

25. Bristol Parish Vestry Book, Virginia State Library.

26. Weisiger, Benjamin B., III, "Prince George County, Virginia, Wills & Deeds 1713-1728", 1973.

27. Boddie, John B., "Historical Southern Families", Vol 5, p 296.

# T0100000 - FRANCIS TUCKER

## (THE ELDER)

### MD MARY ____

CHARLES CITY CO., VA. [1]

Charles City County is one of the eight original counties of Virginia. It has been considered one of the burned record counties. However, fragments of some order books have been extracted by Weisiger, and include the following pertaining to the subject Francis Tucker the Elder.

p242, ca 1689, Adm. gr. Fra. Tucker on estate of Warner Coleman decd, and Jarvis Dix and Francies Coleman give bond. Ord. that est. of Warner & John Coleman, decd, be delivered to Francis Tucker, Admr. of Warner Coleman. Robt. Coleman, who is possessed with those estates, submits to this order in court.

*NOTE: Francis Tucker was at least age 21 when he was named as administrator of Warner Coleman's estate in 1689 in Charles City Co. so he must have been born at least as early as 1668, for his son John was probably b c1691.*

*NOTE: The above administration implies there may be some relationship between Francis Tucker and Warner Coleman. Was Francis Tucker's wife Mary a Coleman? Or did they have a son or daughter who married a Coleman? We do know that Francis Tucker Sr (c1699-1777), son of subject Francis the Elder had a daughter Prudence who married a Coleman. We also know that Capt. Robert Tucker Sr. (c1677-1750) had a son Robert Tucker Jr (c1706-1769) who married Frances Coleman, dau of William Coleman Sr & wf Faith. See "Tucker Trails Through Southside Virginia", a history of Capt Robert Tucker Sr & his descendants, compiled 1986 by B. DeRoy Beale.*

The relationship, if any, between Francis Tucker the Elder (c1668-1723) and Capt Robert Tucker Sr (c1677-1750) is not clear. Other Tuckers who patented land early in the 1700s in Prince George Co, included William (b before 1691), Joseph (b before 1691) and Daniel (b before 1701, who were known to be brothers. They were contemporaries of Francis and Robert and all may have been brothers, but there is not enough evidence for proof.

p409, ca 1692, New Grand Jury called over; Thomas Anderson, foreman, among names sworn, Fran. Tucker.

p416, ca Sept 1692, Francis Tucker failed to appear at court, re: orphans, and to be taken into custody by Sher. to give security that he (and others) will have the orphans at next court.

p423, ca. Oct 1692, Case of Wm. Epes, Jr., agst Richard Bland for Bland's refusal to pay him 400 lbs. tobacco won in a horse race, referred to jury for trial.

p424, The Jury is: Henry Harman, foreman; Lambert Tye, Fran. Tucker, John Makeny, Wm. Laws, who find for deft.

p426, ca. Oct 1692, Judgment gr. Robert Tucker agst. Francis Tucker, for 1717 lbs. tobacco.

p450, ca. 1693. These persons fined by grand jury for non-appearance: Fran. Tucker, James Samon, Lewis Green, Barth. Jackson & John Myles.

p503, ca. June 1694, Francis Tucker & his wife, summoned as wit. for John Golightly, are ea. fined 300 lbs. tobo. for not appearing, unless they give a good excuse.

p507, ca 3 Aug 1694, Francis Tucker & wife give sufficient excuse for not attending as wit. for John Golightly.

PRINCE GEORGE CO. VA. [2]

In 1703, Prince George Co. was formed from that part of Charles City Co. lying south of the James River. Prince George County is one of Virginia's "burned counties", but some records which survived were extracted by Weisiger and include the following references to the subject Francis Tucker the Elder.

p750, Survey, 21 May 1712, Francis Tucker on b.s. of

Mawhipponoak Cr., 289 ac. *(See Patent 10-339.)*

p750, Survey, 22 May 1712, Francis Tucker on w.s. of Mawhipponoak Cr., 100 ac. *(A patent could not be found for this 100 ac. but see Deed, p 231.)*

p118, Deed, Aug 14, 1716, Geo. Crooke of Bristol Parish, Pr. Geo. Co. to David Crawley for 11 lbs., 289 ac., 100 ac. part of gr. by patent to Hugh Lee, Sr., & by him to John Golightly and by Golightly sold to Solomon Crook, adj. Isaac Colson, John Golightly, Francis Tucker; part of gr. to Hugh Lee, Sr., etc. late in tenure of Richard Smith and by Smith sold to Solomon Crook. Another tract of 89 ac. next to Robert Burgess, Mr. Coleman, Gagley's Meadow, Hugh Lee, etc. S/ George Crooke. Wit: John x Browder, Peter x Overby, Chas. Roberts. Rec. Aug 14, 1716. Elizabeth, wife of Geo. Crooke, ack. dower.

p 231, Deed, Jun 10, 1718. Francis Tucker The Elder, of Bristol Par., Pr. Geo. Co., to David Crawley of the same, 100 ac. bo. by land of sd. Crawley, Edmond Browder, land late in possession of Bartholomew Crowder, John Butler. S/ Francis x Tucker. Wit: Henry Randolph Jr., E. Goodrich, John Patteson. Rec. Jun 10, 1718. Mary, wife of sd Francis Tucker, ack. dower.

p 663, Will of Francis Tucker of Bristol Parish, d 12 Dec 1722, p 10 Dec 1723.
son, Francis, land on n.e. side of Mawhipponoak Cr. lower end.
son John, land n.s. same creek, joining Henry Mayes.
son Henry, land bet. sons Francis & John, inc. plantation where I now live.
son Abram, land n.s. Mawhipponoak Cr. joining son Henry & Thomas Mitchell.
son Mathew, land joining Thomas Mitchell.
All goods to be equally divided bet. children & wife Mary.
Wit: Mathew Mayes, Henry Mayes, John Powell.
S/ Francis x Tucker.

p 915, Aug 9, 1726. Inv. of certain particulars of Francis Tucker's est. by Francis (T) Tucker, Adm'r.

PATENT [3]

Patent 10-339, 15 Jul 1717 Frances Tucker Sr., 289 ac. NL Pr. Geo. Co. on b.s. Mawhipponock Cr., adj. Herbert's line, 30 sh.

*NOTE: The lands which Francis Tucker the Elder patented on b.s. Mawhipponock Cr. and willed to his sons, lay in the area which was separated from Prince George Co. in 1752 to form Dinwiddie Co, and only fragmented records remain for either county. Just how many acres he willed to each son is unknown. However, see separate chapters for each son.*

SUMMARY:

Francis Tucker the Elder b ca 1668, lived in Charles City Co., d 1723 in Prince George Co., md Mary _____, probably in Charles City Co. ca 1690, and had issue:

John Tucker, Sr., b ca 1691

Francis Tucker Sr., b ca 1699

Matthew Tucker, Sr., b ca 1699

Henry Tucker, b ca 1707

Abram Tucker, b ca 1719

1. Weisiger, Benjamin B. III, "Charles City County, Virginia Court Orders 1687-1695", 1984
2. Weisiger, Benjamin B. III, "Prince George County, Virginia Wills & Deeds 1713-1728", 1973
3. Card File of Land Patents and Grants, Virginia State Library Archives.

# T0110000 - FRANCIS TUCKER SR

## MD ANN _____

## SON OF FRANCIS TUCKER (THE ELDER)

## MD MARY _____

PRINCE GEORGE CO. VA. [1]

p663, Will of Francis Tucker of Bristol Parish, d 12 Dec 1722, p 10 Dec 1723.

son, Francis, land on n.e. side of Mawhipponoak Cr. lower end.

son John, land n.s. same creek, joining Henry Mayes.

son Henry, land bet. sons Francis & John, inc. plantation where I now live.

son Abram, land n.s. Mawhipponoak Cr. joining son Henry & Thomas Mitchell.

son Mathew, land joining Thomas Mitchell.

All goods to be equally divided bet. children & wife Mary.

Wit: Mathew Mayes, Henry Mayes, John Powell.

S/ Francis x Tucker

p 915, Aug 9, 1726. Inv. of certain particulars of Francis Tucker's est. by Francis (T) Tucker, Adm'r.

> *NOTE: The lands which Francis Tucker the Elder willed to his sons lay in the area which was separated from Pr. Geo. Co. in 1752 to form Dinwiddie Co., and only fragmented records remain for either county.*

p 1024, Survey, 21 Mar 1726. Francis Tucker on b.s. of Winticomake Cr., 392 ac. *(See Patent 13-461.)*

p 1022, Deed, 11 Jul 1727, Patrick Dorum of Pr., Geo. Co. to William Chambers of Henrico Co., for L15, 100 ac. on w.s. of Mawhipponoak Cr. in Pr. Geo Co. bo. Henry Mays' line and adj. Francis Tucker.

PATENTS [2]

Patent 13-461, 28 Sep 1730, Francis Tucker, Pr. Geo. Co., 392 ac. b.s. of Wintocomaick Cr., adj. Charles Judkins. *(See Survey in*

*Prince George Co.)*

Patent 17-448, 2 Jan 1737, Francis Tucker, Amelia Co. Va. 400 ac., b.s. of Great Br. of Wintocomaick Cr.,, adj. his own, Robert Bolling's & Wm. Coleman's lines.

*NOTE: See Summary of Land Transactions.*

BRISTOL PARISH REGISTER [3]

Amy dau of Francis & Anne Tucker born 12th May last bapt July 9th 1721.

Fran: son of Fran: & Anne Tucker born 1st Nov last bapt 7th Nov 1723.

John son of Frances and Ann Tucker born 25th June bapt 28th septr 1726.

ann D of francis and ann Tucker Born 19th febr Bapt 19th March 1729.

Martha Dr of Francis & ann Tucker Born 21th febr 1732 Bapt march 3d.

*NOTE: Since the subject Francis Tucker Sr was a parent as early as 1721, he was married probably ca 1720 at age 21, and was born probably ca 1699.*

AMELIA CO. VA.

1735, Amelia Co. was formed from that part of Pr. Geo. Co., which lay north and west (upper side) of Numiseen Cr. The area on both sides of Wintocomaick Cr. is now included in Amelia Co.

DB 1-153, 11 Aug 1738. John x Parish to Edward Parish for L114.10, 150 ac. s.s. of Wintocomake Cr., below main upper fork, bo. in part by Francis Tucker's line and Gr. Br.

DB 1-189, 7 Jul 1739. Francis Tucker to Thomas Hood for L20., 300 ac. pt. of tract b.s. Gr. Br. of Wintocomaic Cr., bo. Bollings line & a sm. spr. bt.. Ann, wife of Francis ack. dower int. Wit: John Powell, Daniel Coleman & James Clark. Rec. 7 Jul 1739. *(See Patents 13-461 & 17-448.)*

DB 1-190, 16 Jul 1739. Francis x Tucker to Abraham Crowder of Pr. Geo. Co., for consideration of 1 shilling. Lease of, 50 ac. u.s. Winticomick Cr. bet Bevil's lines & adj. sd Abraham Crowder's lines & sd cr. Wit: William Watson & Lodwick Tanner.
*(See Release following.)*

DB 1-191, 17 Jul 1739. Deed of Release. Francis x Tucker to Abraham Crowder of Pr. Geo. Co., consid. L10. Wit: Wm. Watson, Lodwick Tanner. 50 ac. described in preceding Deed of Lease. Rec. 20 Jul 1739, Ann, wife of Francis Tucker ack. dower.
*(See Patents 13-461 & 17-448.)*

DB 1-307, 2 Jan 1740. Edward Parish to Henry Talley for L20., 150 ac. pt. of greater tract s.s. Wintocomack Cr. below main upper fk. bo. in pt. by Francis Tucker's line, the Gr. Br. of the Cr. Wit: Sarah x Tucker, Mary x Powell John Powell.

> *NOTE: The identity of Sarah Tucker as a witness to above deed is uncertain. She may be Sarah Old wife of a John Tucker Sr (not subject Francis' brother), who inherited land on 1.s. Wintocomake Cr. from his father Capt. Robert Tucker Sr.*

DB 3-61, 18 May 1748, Fran. Tucker to Matthew Tucker for L17, 100 ac. bo. Thomas Hood's line, Fran. Tucker's line, Peter Coleman's line, Godfrey Coleman's line, Crawley's line. Wit: Parmonas Palmer, William Palmer, William (H) Hood.
*(See Patents 13-461 & 17-448.)*

DB 5-231, 17 Dec 1754, Francis Tucker (Sr?), for love, good will & affection for loving son Francis Tucker (Jr), 50 ac. on s.s. of Wintocomake Cr., joining the plantation whereon he now lives. Wit: Richard Talley, Jr. S/.Francis (T) Tucker.

DB 5-232, 17 Dec 1754, Francis Tucker Sr,. for love, good will & affection to loving son John Tucker, 70 ac. on s.s. of Wintocomake Cr., bo. Richard Talley's line, up Cr. to his brother Francis' line. Wit: Richard (R) Talley, Matthew (M) Tucker, William (H) Hood. S/ Francis (T)Tucker.
*(See Patents 13-461 & 17-448.)*

DB 9-47. 24 Sep 1766, Francis Tucker Sen & wf Ann to Matthew Tucker Jun, for L8, 16 ac. on Horsepen Br. on Abram Hood's line, sd Matthew Tucker's Spring Br. & line. Wit: Henry (x) Tucker, Thomas (x) Tucker, Wm. Hall. Rec. 25 Sep 1766. S/ Francis (x) Tucker, Ann (x) Tucker. *(See Patents 13-461 & 17-448.)*

DB 8-166, 16 Jun 1763, John Tucker to Francis Tucker, for L400 (or L500), 14 cattle with a cross of half moon in their right ear, a Bay Horse & Sorrel Mare, 15 hogs, 3 beds, 2 chests, a parcel of pewter, 2 pots & all other estate the sd John Tucker hath any right or title in. Wit: Absolom Tucker, Francis Tucker. Rec. 23 Jun 1763. S/ John (x) Tucker.

DB13-76, 4 Jun 1774, Francis Tucker for L5, & love & affection for son John Tucker, 2 horses, 10 head cattle, 2 beds of furniture, 2 iron pots, 1 doz. pewter plates, 4 doz. head hogs. S/ Francis (x) Tucker. Rec. 27 Oct 1774. Wit: Edmund Wills, Absolom Tucker, Matthew (x) Tucker, Francis (x) Tucker Jr.

DB 13-158, 10 Nov 1774, Samuel Morgan Jun. & wf Mary, and John Morgan & wf Mary, to Absolom Tucker, for L125, 300 ac. on u.s. of Wintocomake Cr., bo. Wills' line, John Clancy's line. Wit: Peter Lamkin, Charles Irby, Wm. Crenshaw, Wm. Doswell. Rec. 27 Apr 1775. S/ Samuel Morgan, Mary Morgan, John Morgan, Mary Morgan. *(See DB 13-181.)*

DB 13-181, 20 Oct 1774, Francis Tucker Senior & Absolom Tucker & Wife Susannah, to John Morgan for L25, & further consideration of, 300 ac. in Raleigh Parish, this day conveyed unto Absolom by sd John --- Francis Tucker, Absolom Tucker & wf Susannah, sold to John Morgan 177 ac., 1.s. Wintocomake being all the land which the sd Francis Tucker lately possessed & which he hath given to his son Absolom Tucker, bo. mouth of Horsepen Br. on Wintocomake Cr., Elias Witt's line, John Wilson's line, John Tucker's line, Abram Hood's line, Horsepen Br., Matthew Tucker's Sp. Br., a second Br. Wit: Francis Tucker Jun, Simon Morgan, Edmd Wils. Rec. 27 Apr 1775. S/ Francis (x) Tucker Sen, Absolom (x) Tucker, Susannah (x) Tucker. *(See DB 13-158 of Absolom Tucker.)*

WB 2-207, will of Francis Tucker Sr. wd Jun 6, 1774, wp (date not shown).

Exec. Son Francis Tucker.

Leg: Grandson Francis Tucker - furniture.

Absolom Tucker - furniture.

Amy Hastains - bed.

Son Absolom Tucker - chairs.

Son Francis Tucker - negro Joe, all the rest of my estate.

Son John Tucker - one shilling sterling.

Dau. Prudence Coleman - one shilling sterling.

Dau. Pressillo Walker - one shilling sterling.

(no land was mentioned) (date recorded was not shown).

WB 2-218, Francis Tucker Est. I&A dated Feb 26, 1777 (date recorded not shown). Appr: George Worsham, Joseph Crowder & Henry Tucker. Adm. Francis Tucker. Value L78.15.9.

*(Note: From above Est I&A, it is assumed that Francis Tucker Sr. died in 1777.)*

LIST OF TITHABLES

| 1736 | 1 | Francis Tucker | |
|------|---|----------------|---|
| 1737 | 1 | Francis Tucker | |
| 1738 | 1 | Francis Tucker | |
| 1739 | 1 | Francis Tucker | |
| 1740 | 2 | Francis Tucker Sr & Jr | |
| 1741 | 2 | Francis Tucker Senr, Francis Tucker | |
| 1744 | | Francis Tucker Senr, Francis Tucker Jun, John Tucker | |
| 1747 | 3 | Francis Tucker, Francis Tucker, John Tucker | |
| 1750 | | Francis Tucker Sr | |
| 1751 | 2 | Francis Tucker | Joe |
| 1752 | 2 | Francis Tucker | Joe |
| 1753 | 2 | Francis Tucker | Joe |
| 1755 | 2 | Francis Tucker | Joe |
| 1756 | 2 | Francis Tucker | Joe |
| 1762 | 2 | Francis Tucker | Joe |

## LIST OF TITHABLES

| 1763 | 3 | 200 | Francis Tucker Sen, Absolom Tucker | Joe |
| 1765 | 3 | 76 | Francis Tucker Sen., Absolom Tucker | Joe |
| 1767 | 3 | 177 | Francis Tucker Sen, Absolom Tucker | Joe |
| 1769 | 2 | ---- | Francis Tucker Sen | Joe |
| 1770 | 2 | 177 | Francis Tucker | Joe |

*(See WB 2-209, 1774, Francis Tucker.)*

## SUMMARY OF LAND TRANSACTIONS IN AMELIA CO.

| YR | REF | REC | DISP | BAL |
|----|-----|-----|------|-----|
| 1730 | Pat. 13-461 | 392 | | 392 |
| 1737 | Pat. 17-448 | 400 | | 792 |
| 1739 | DB 1-189 to Thomas Hood | | 300 | 492 |
| 1739 | DB 1-191 to Abraham Crowder | | 50 | 442 |
| 1748 | DB 3-61 to Matthew Tucker | | 100 | 342 |
| 1754 | DB 5-231 to son Francis Tucker Jr | | 50 | 292 |
| 1754 | DB 5-232 to son John Tucker | | 70 | 222 |
| 1766 | DB 9-47 to Matthew Tucker Jr | | 16 | 206 |
| 1774 | DB 13-181 to John Morgan | | 177 | 29 |
| | Totals | 792 | 763 | |

*There is a discrepancy of 29 ac. btwn the 792 ac. received and 763 ac. disposed. In the tax record, Francis Tucker Sen owned 200 ac. in 1763 and 177 ac. in 1776, a difference of 23 ac. This compiler has been unable to reconcile the differences.*

SUMMARY:

Francis Tucker Sr, son of Francis Tucker the Elder & wf Mary, b ca 1699 in Charles City Co., d 1777 in Amelia Co., md Ann ca 1720 in Prince George Co., and had issue:

Amy Tucker b 1721, md ___ Hastains.

Francis Tucker Jr. b1723.

John Tucker b 1726, md ___ Martha.

Ann Tucker b 1729.

Martha Tucker b 1732, md _____ Tucker Tally, son of Richard Tally.

Absolom Tucker b ca 1747, md ____Susannah ____ .

Prudence Tucker, b ____ md ____ Coleman.

Pressillo Tucker, b ____ md ____ Walker.

1. Weisiger, Benjamin B. III, "Prince George County, Virginia Wills & Deeds 1713-1728", 1973
2. Card File of Land Patents and Grants, Virginia State Library Archives
3. Boddie, John B., "Births 1720-1792 from the Bristol Parish Register of Henrico, Prince George and Dinwiddie."

# T0111000 - FRANCIS TUCKER JR

## MD MARTHA HUDDLESTON

## SON OF FRANCIS TUCKER SR

### MD ANN _____

BRISTOL PARISH REGISTER [1]

Fran: son of Fran: & Anne Tucker born 1st Nov last bapt 7th Nov 1723.

AMELIA CO. VA.

DB 5-231, 17 Dec 1754, Francis Tucker (Sr?), for love, good will & affection for loving son Francis Tucker (Jr?), 50 ac. on s.s. of Wintocomake Cr., joining the plantation whereon he now lives. Wit: Richard Talley, Jr. S/ Francis (T) Tucker.

WB 2-207, will of Francis Tucker Sr. wd Jun 6, 1774, wp (date not shown).
Exec. Son Francis Tucker.
Leg: Grandson Francis Tucker - furniture.
Absolom Tucker - furniture.
Amy Hastains - bed.
Son Absolom Tucker - chairs.
Son Francis Tucker - negro Joe, all the rest of my estate.
Son John Tucker - one shilling sterling.
Dau. Prudence Coleman - one shilling sterling.
Dau. Pressillo Walker - one shilling sterling.
(no land was mentioned) (date recorded was not shown).

WB 2-218, Francis Tucker Est. I&A dated Feb 26, 1777 (date recorded not shown). Appr: George Worsham, Joseph Crowder & Henry Tucker. Adm: Francis Tucker. Value L78.15.9.

*NOTE: From above Est I&A, it is assumed that Francis Tucker Sr. died in 1777.*

MARRIAGE BOND

4 Aug 1784, Francis Tucker to Martha Huddleston Sec. Robert Crowder.

## LIST OF TITHABLES

| 1740-1747 | | Francis Tucker Jr listed as 16-yr-up tithable in household of his father Francis Tucker Sr. (but Bristol Parish Register says he was b 1723) |
|---|---|---|
| 1744 | 1 | Fran Tucker Jr, Dilce |
| 1747 | 2 | Francis Tucker, ____ |
| 1749 | 1 | Francis Tucker Jun |
| 1750 | 1 | Francis Tucker Jun |
| 1752 | 1 | Francis Tucker Jur |
| 1753 | 1 | Francis Tucker Jun |
| 1762 | 1 | Francis Tucker son of Francis Tucker |
| 1763 | 1-75 | Francis Tucker Jun |
| 1765 | 3-75 | Francis Tucker, Denson Walker, Samuel Vaughan |
| 1767 | 1-75 | Francis Tucker |
| 1769 | 1-__ | Francis Tucker Jun |
| 1770 | 2-75 | Francis Tucker, Zock, Harting |

## PERSONAL TAX RECORDS

| 1782 | 4 | Francis Tucker (Boatswain), Joe, Jude |
|---|---|---|
| 1783 | 3 | Francis Tucker |
| 1784 | 3 | Francis Tucker |
| 1786 | 1 | Francis Tucker |
| 1787 | 1 | Francis Tucker |
| 1788 | 1 | Francis Tucker |
| 1789 | 1 | Francis Tucker |
| 1790 | 1 | Francis Tucker |
| 1791 | 1 | Francis Tucker |

*(See WB 5-1, 1792, Francis Tucker.)*

## LAND TAX RECORDS

1782-1792 Francis Tucker, 75 ac.

*NOTE: In 1754, (DB 5-231) Francis Tucker Sr gave to his son Francis Tucker Jr 50 ac. of land. Personal Tax Records show Francis Tucker Jr with 75 ac. in 1763-70, and Land Tax Records show him holding 75 ac. 1782-92. Where he obtained the additional 25 ac. is not determined.*

WB 5-1, wd 14 Oct 1792, wp 28 Mar 1793, will of Francis Tucker. Wit: Jeremiah Tanner, Blanch x Tanner, Robert x Talley. Exs: beloved wife (not named) & friends Thomas T. Wells & Robert Tanner. Leg: to Herod Croudex (?)(perhaps Crowder) - 2 hephers. to beloved wife (not named) - the land & plantation whereon I now live; plus negro man Joe, stock, horses, cattle, hogs & all other stock, household & kitchen furniture & plantation tools. S/ Francis Tucker.

*NOTE: The above will seems to be that of Francis Tucker Jr, son of Francis Tucker Sr.*

DB 19-262. 10 Apr 1793, Martha Tucker to John Morgan Sen., for L25, 75 ac. on s.s. of Wintocomake Cr., formerly the property of Francis Tucker decd, bo. Matthew Wills, Henry Tucker's line. Wit: Thos. T. Wells, Henry x Tucker, Elizabeth x Tucker. S/ Martha Tucker.

*NOTE: Although Francis Tucker Jr did not identify his wife by name in his will above, the Marriage Bond and the DB 19-262 above identify her as Martha Huddleston.*

*NOTE: The identity of Herod Crowder named in the will of Francis Tucker Jr is not clear.*

The Personal Tax Records for Francis Tucker Jr never include a 16-yr-up white tithable in his household. But the Personal Tax Records show as a separate household, one white tithable, Herod Crowder Tucker in 1787, and Herod C. Tucker 1788-91.

The Land Tax Records show 1788 alterations Herod Crowder Tucker d of Jno Phipps 30 ac., and Herod Crowder Tucker holding 30 ac. 1789-92. They show Herod T. Crowder holding 30+20+10 ac. 1795, 30+30 ac. 1797, 60 (or 68) ac. 1798, 68 ac. 1800-07, 68+29 ac. 1809, 97 ac. 1810-13, 162 ac. 1815-1818, the 97 ac. being adj. George Kidd & Joel Bevill.

It appears Herod Crowder Tucker, Herod C. Tucker and Herod T. Crowder may be one and the same person, with a unique relationship to Francis Tucker Jr, as a legatee in his will.

*NOTE: Francis Tucker Sr in his will (WB 2-207, 1774) named "my grandson Francis Tucker", but Francis Tucker Jr did not name a son Francis in his will (WB 5-1, 1793). The grandson is most probably Francis Tucker b 1772, son of Absolom Tucker & wf Susannah.*

*NOTE: In 1770, there were three Francis Tuckers listed in the tax records.*

*1770 2-177 Francis Tucker, Joe (probably Francis Sr, 1699-1777)*

*1770 2-75 Francis Tucker, Zock, Harding (probably Francis Jr 1723-1793)*

*1770 6-275 Francis Tucker, Godfrey Tucker (Patroller), Dick, Harry, Jiram, _____*

*(probably Francis b 1726, the orphaned son of John Tucker Sr and nephew of Francis Tucker Sr, who in 1741 (DB 1-531) chose William Traylor as his guardian).*

*The Godfrey Tucker is most probably son of Robert Tucker Jr., who, inherited 275 1/2 ac. from his father in 1768 (WB 2X-283) and sold 275 ac. in 1782 (DB 16-227)).*

SUMMARY:

This subject Francis Tucker Jr., son of Francis Tucker Sr & wf Ann, born 1723 in Prince George Co., died 1793 in Amelia Co., md 1782 in Amelia Co., Martha Huddleston.

Whether they had issue is uncertain.

Herod Crowder Tucker (Herod T. Crowder) may have been a son or foster son or nephew.

1. Boddie, John B., "Births, 1720-1792 from the Bristol Parish Register of Henrico, Prince George and Dinwiddie."

# T0112000 - JOHN TUCKER

## MD MARTHA _____
## SON OF FRANCIS TUCKER SR
## MD ANN _____

BRISTOL PARISH REGISTER [1]

John son of Francis and Ann Tucker born 25th June bapt 28th Septr 1726.

AMELIA CO. VA.

LIST OF TITHABLES

| 1744-47 | | John Tucker listed as 16-yr-up tithable in household of his father Francis Tucker |
|---|---|---|
| 1749 | 1 | John Tucker |
| 1750 | 1 | John Tucker |
| 1751 | 1 | John Tucker |
| 1755 | 1 | John Tucker |
| 1762 | 1 | John Tucker |
| 1763 | 1 | John Tucker |
| 1767 | 1-190 | John Tucker |
| 1769 | 1-___ | John Tucker |
| 1769 | 1-190 | Daniel Tucker son of John |
| 1770 | 1-190 | Daniel Tucker son of John |

LAND TAX RECORDS

| 1782-1804 | John Tucker, 190 ac. |
|---|---|
| 1805 | Martha Tucker, 190 ac. |
| 1806-1807 | Abel Tucker, 190 ac. |
| 1809-1810 | Abel Tucker, 190+193 ac. |
| 1811-1812 | Abel Tucker, 383 ac. |
| 1813-1814 | Abel Tucker, 195 ac. |
| 1815 | William Tucker, deed from Abel, 195 ac. |

*NOTE: John Tucker was listed as a 16-yr-up tithable in the household of his father Francis Tucker, Sr in 1744 and 1747. In 1749 he was listed as a separate household 21-yr-old. This conforms with his birthdate in 1726 as recorded in the Bristol Parish Register. He became age 16 in 1742, and age 21 in 1747.*

DB 5-232, 17 Dec 1754, Francis Tucker Sr. for love, good will & affection to loving son John Tucker, 70 ac. on s.s. of Wintocomake Cr., bo. Richard Talley's line, up cr. to his brother Francis' line. Wit: Richard (R) Talley, Matthew (M) Tucker, William (H) Hood. S/ Francis (T) Tucker. *(See DB 8-198.)*

DB 8-166, 16 Jun 1763, John Tucker to Francis Tucker, for L400.(or L500), 14 cattle with a cross of half moon in their right ear, a Bay Horse & Sorrel Mare, 15 hogs, 3 beds, 2 chests, a parcel of pewter, 2 pots & all other estate the sd John Tucker hath any right or title in. Wit: Absolom Tucker, Francis Tucker. Rec. 23 Jun 1763.
S/ John (x) Tucker.

DB 8-198, 7 May 1763, John Tucker, son of Francis Tucker of Raleigh Parish, to Richard Talley Jr., for L30, 70 ac. on Wintocomake Cr., bo. sd. Cr. & mouth of small spring br. in Richard Talley's line, Francis Tucker Jun's line, line btwn. sd. John Tucker & Francis Tucker Jun., made by Francis Tucker Sen, father of sd John. Wit: Hezekiah Coleman, Richard (x) Talley, Tucker (x) Talley. Rec. 22 Sep 1763. S/ John (x) Tucker *(See DB 5-232.)*

DB 9-190, 10 Aug 1767, David Cowley to John Tucker for L55, 190 ac. bo. Francis Tucker's & Abraham Crowder's lines, Abraham Hood's line, Tisdale's line, John Wilson's line. Rec. 27 Aug 1767. Wife Elizabeth relinq dower. S/ David (x) Cowley, Eliza.

*(See Land Tax Records, and see DB 22-391.)*

*NOTE: The above deed indicates John Tucker, Francis Tucker, Abraham Crowder, Abraham Hood were neighbors*

DB 13-76, 4 Jun 1774, Francis Tucker for L5, & love & affection for son John Tucker, 2 horses, 10 head cattle, 2 beds of furniture, 2 iron pots, 1 doz. pewter plates, 4 doz. head hogs. S/ Francis (x) Tucker. Rec. 27 Oct 1774. Wit: Edmund Wills, Absolom Tucker,

Matthew (x) Tucker, Francis (x) Tucker Jr.

WB 2-207, will of Francis Tucker Sr, wd Jun 6, 1774, wp (date not shown).
Exec: Son Francis Tucker.
Leg: Grandson Francis Tucker - furniture.
Absolom Tucker - furniture.
Amy Hastains - bed.
Son Absolom Tucker - chairs.
Son Francis Tucker - negro Joe, all the rest of my estate.
Son John Tucker - one shilling sterling.
Dau. Prudence Coleman - one shilling sterling.
Dau. Pressillo Walker - one shilling sterling.
    (no land was mentioned) (date recorded was not shown).

WB 2-218, Francis Tucker Est. I&A dated Feb 26, 1777 (date recorded not shown). Appr: George Worsham, Joseph Crowder & Henry Tucker. Adm. Francis Tucker. Value L78.15.9.

*(Note: From above Est I&A, it is assumed that Francis Tucker Sr. died in 1777).*

*NOTE: The John and Shadrick Tucker in the following two deeds DB 18-44, and will WB 5-472, are sons of John Tucker & wife Martha, who married Fanny & Rachael Hood, daughters of John Hood & wf Catherine.*

DB 18-44. 4 Aug 1786, John Hood to John Tucker for love & good will & affection I have for John Tucker, one negro girl Amey. Wit: Samuel Morgan, John x Tucker, Abraham x Tucker. S/ John Hood. Rec 28 Dec 1786.

DB 18-44, 4 Aug 1786, John Hood to Shadrick Tucker, for love, good will & affection I have for Shadrick Tucker - one negro girl Saray. Wit: Samuel Morgan, John Tucker, Absolom Tucker. S/ John Hood.

WB 5-472, 16 Apr 1789, wp 26 Apr 1798, will of John Hood, of Amelia Co.
Wife Catherine Hood - such maintenance as my executors think reasonable.

William Hood - 5 shillings sterling.

son Thomas Hood - 3 negroes Peter, Jack & Sam & that part of my land lying in the fork of the branch where he now lives.

dau Mary Hood - negro girl Nell & incr. & L30.

dau Fanny Tucker, wf of John Tucker- 5 shillings sterling.

dau. Rahab (Rachael?) Tucker, wf of Shadrack Tucker - 5 shillings sterling.

son Edward Hood, the whole of land where I now live, below the line already mentioned to son Thomas.

son Edward - remainder part of my est. be it of what nature or kind soever paying regard that if my son Edward should die without heir, his part be div. btwn his bro. Thomas & sister Mary., & if dau Mary die without heir, her part to go to her bro Edward Hood.

Exor. Matthew Tucker, William Walthall, Millington Roach, Thomas Hood, Joseph Bevill & William Wilson.

Wit: Paschall Tucker, Elizabeth x Tucker, Matthew x Tucker, Nancy x Reess(?).

WB 7-115. will of John Tucker wd 6 Mar 1797, wp 26 Jul 1804, Leg: to wife Martha - plantation where I now live - plus 3 negroes Dick, Luis, & Aggy, horses, hogs, cattle, household & furniture & residue, for life or widowhood, & afterwards equally divided among my children Abel Tucker, my land (?), John Tucker, Shadrack Tucker, Ezekiahr Tucker. Ex: Absolom Tucker, Thomas Tucker, John Hood. Wit: Robert Tanner, Elam Tanner, Patsey Tanner. *(See DB 22-391 for 193 ac..)*

WB 7-330, 8 Oct 1805, Rec 23 Jul 1807, I&A Est. of John Tucker. Included no slaves. Total value L63.7.2.

WB 7-331, Oct 8, 1805, Acct of Sale of Est. of John Tucker. L60.14.1 1/2.

DB 22-391, 20 Oct 1807, Marthey Tucker to son Abel Tucker, for natural love & affection, 193 ac. being land sd Marthey now lives on, bo. Abraham Hood, Richard Cardwell, & land formerly property of Andrew Vaughan. S/ Marthey Tucker. Wit: Joshua Eppes, Branch Tucker.

*(Note: Marthey Tucker was most probably Martha Tucker,*

*widow of John Tucker, and Abel Tucker was their son.)*

*(See DB 9-190 where John Tucker purchased this land.)*

DB 24-86, 18 Nov 1814, rec 25 May 1815, Abel Tucker of Charlotte Co., to William Tucker of Amelia Co., for $780., 195 ac. bo. Richard Cardwell, Solomon Hood, Abraham Hood, est of Andrew Waugh, decd. S/ Abel x Tucker. Wit: G. Cardwell, Abraham Tucker, Boswell x Tucker.

> *NOTE: The List of Tithables show John Tucker holding 190 ac. in 1767, but then show "Daniel Tucker son of John" holding the 190 ac. in 1769-70. This is the only reference found of Daniel Tucker son of John, and he is not named in the will of his father, John Tucker son of Francis Sr & Ann. The Land Tax Records indicate that John Tucker held the 190 ac. from 1782 until his death in 1804, then passed to his widow Martha in 1805, then to his son Abel in 1806.*

SUMMARY: John Tucker, son of Francis Tucker Sr & wf Ann, b 1726 Prince George Co., d 1804 Amelia Co., and Martha, & had issue:

Daniel Tucker b ca 1748.

Abel Tucker b ca 1761.

Shadrack Tucker b ca 1761, m Rachael Hood, dau of John Hood.⁻

Ezekiahr Tucker b ca 1764.

John Tucker b ca 1765, m Fanny Hood, dau of John Hood.

# T0112100a - DANIEL TUCKER

## SON OF JOHN TUCKER

## MD MARTHA

*[This Daniel Tucker chapter and associated line were part of the 1986 research of the Francis Tucker line by B. DeRoy Beale. See chapter T0112100b and the associated family line for later thoughts Mr. Beale developed on this descendant.]*

AMELIA CO. VA.

DB 9-190, 10 Aug 1767, David Cowley to John Tucker for L55, 190 ac bo Francis Tucker's & Abraham Crowder's lines, Abraham Hood's line, Tisdale's line, John Wilson's line. Rec. 27 Aug 1767. Wife Elizabeth relinq dower. S/ David (x) Cowley, Eliza.

LIST OF TITHABLES

1767 1-190 John Tucker

1769 1-190 Daniel Tucker, son of John

1770 1-190 Daniel Tucker, son of John

> *NOTE: The List of Tithables show John Tucker holding 190 ac. in 1767, but then show "Daniel Tucker son of John" holding the 190 ac. in 1769-70. This is the only reference found of Daniel Tucker son of John, and he is not named will of his father, John Tucker son of Francis Sr & Ann. The Land Tax Records indicate that John Tucker held the 190 ac. from 1782 until his death in 1804, then passed to his widow Martha in 1805, then to his son Abel in 1806.*

WB 7-115. will of John Tucker, wd 6 Mar 1797, wp 26 Jul 1804, Leg: to wife Martha - plantation where I now live - plus 3 negroes Dick, Luis, & Aggy, horses, hogs, cattle, household & furniture & residue, for life or widowhood, & afterwards equally divided among my children Abel Tucker, my land (?), John Tucker, Shadrack Tucker, Ezekiahr Tucker.
Ex: Absolom Tucker, Thomas Tucker, John Hood.
Wit: Robert Tanner, Elam Tanner, Patsey Tanner.

SUMMARY:

If Daniel Tucker, son of John & Martha Tucker, was age 21 when he first held the 190 ac. in 1769, he would have been born ca 1748.

Nothing more about this Daniel Tucker is known by this compiler.

# T0112200a - ABEL TUCKER

## SON OF JOHN TUCKER

## MD MARTHA __

AMELIA CO. VA.

WB 7-115. will of John Tucker, wd 6 Mar 1797, wp 26 Jul 1804, Leg: to Wife Martha - plantation where I now live - plus 3 negroes Dick, Luis, & Aggy, horses, hogs, cattle, household & furniture & residue, for life or widowhood, & afterwards equally divided amony my children Abel Tucker, my land (?), John Tucker, Shadrack Tucker, Ezekiahr Tucker. Ex: Absolom Tucker, Thomas Tucker, John Hood. Wit: Robert Tanner, Elam Tanner, Patsey Tanner.

WB 7-330, 8 Oct 1805, Rec 23 Jul 1807, I&A Est. of John Tucker. Included no slaves. Total value L63.7.2.

WB 7-331, Oct 8, 1805, Acct of Sale of Est. of John Tucker. L60.14.1 1/2.

PERSONAL TAX RECORDS

1782 1 Abel Tucker.

LAND TAX RECORDS

1782-1804 John Tucker, 190 ac.
1805 Martha Tucker, 190 ac.
1806-1807 Abel Tucker, 190 ac.
1809-1810 Abel Tucker, 190+193 ac.
1811-1812 Abel Tucker, 383 ac.
1813-1814 Abel Tucker, 195 ac.
1815 William Tucker, deed from Abel, 195 ac.

Abel Tucker was listed on the personal tax records for only one year, in 1782. He was at least age 21 at that time, and would have been born no later than 1761.

John Tucker willed his wife Martha Tucker, 190 ac. for life, then to son Abel. The Land Tax Records show the 190 ac. passing to Martha in 1805, then to Abel who held it beginning in 1806.

However, the Land Tax Records for 1809-1812 are confusing and probably in error. Abel Tucker was already "holding" the 190 ac. in 1806-7, and his mother Martha, who was willed it for life, deeded it, as 193 ac. to Abel in 1807. The 190 ac. & 193 ac. is most probably the same land, which Abel then "held" & sold as 195 ac. in 1814. No other deeds for Abel Tucker could be found in Amelia Co. except the two following:

DB 22-391, 20 Oct 1807, Marthey Tucker to son Abel Tucker, for natural love & affection, 193 ac. being land sd Marthy now lives on, bo. Abraham Hood, Richard Cardwell, & land formerly property of Andrew Vaughan. S/ Marthey Tucker. Wit: Joshua Eppes, Branch Tucker. *(See DB 24-86 for 195 ac.)*

*(Note: The wording "land formerly property of Andrew Vaughan" is confusing. This 193 ac. is most probably the same as 190 ac. which John Tucker purchased of David Cowley in 1767 [DB 9-190], and willed to his wife Martha for life, then to son Abel in 1804 [WB7-115]).*

DB 24-86, 18 Nov 1814, rec 25 May 1815, Abel Tucker of Charlotte Co., to William Tucker of Amelia Co., for $780., 195 ac. bo. Richard Cardwell, Solomon Hood, Abraham Hood, est of Andrew Waugh (Vaughan?) decd. S/ Abel x Tucker. Wit: G. Cardwell, Abraham Tucker, Boswell x Tucker. *(See DB 22-391 for 193 ac.)*

DB 24-191, 20 Jan 1816, rec 22 Feb 1816, William Tucker to Francis Tucker, for $211., 37 ac., bo. widow's dower line, Francis Tucker. S/ William x Tucker. Wit: Thomas T. Wills, Law Wills, William Booth.

*NOTE: The identity of William Tucker in the above two deeds is not clear. The name William does not appear anywhere else in the line of descent from Francis Tucker the Elder (ca 1663-1723). The 37 ac. was bounded by "widow's dower line", and Francis Tucker, but the name of the widow was not shown. In 1815, Abel Tucker, son of John & Martha, sold 195 ac. to William Tucker. It would appear from the Land Tax Records that this 37 ac. is part*

47

*of the 195 ac., for the Land Tax acreage was reduced to 158 ac. But in 1818, the Land Tax Record was corrected back to 196 ac. This would imply that the 37 ac. came from some other source., possibly an inheritance, since there is no deed. There is recorded in Amelia Co. on 22 Jun 1810, the marriage of William Tucker to Sally Tucker, and on 8 Dec 1810 the marriage of Absolom Tucker to Polly Tucker, with Abel Tucker as Security for both marriages. The identity of William, Sally, Absolom & Polly Tucker have not been determined by this compiler.*

SUMMARY:

Abel Tucker, son of John Tucker & wf. Martha, b. in Amelia Co., Va. Moved, in 1815, to Charlotte Co., Va.

This compiler has not further researched Abel Tucker in Charlotte Co., Va.

# T0112300a - JOHN TUCKER

## MD FANNY HOOD
## SON OF JOHN TUCKER
## MD MARTHA _____

AMELIA CO. VA.

DB 18-44. 4 Aug 1786, John Hood to John Tucker for love & good will & affection I have for John Tucker, one negro girl Amey. Wit: Samuel Morgan, John x Tucker, Abraham x Tucker. S/ John Hood. Rec 28 Dec 1786.

DB 18-44, 4 Aug 1786, John Hood to Shadrick Tucker, for love, good will & affection I have for Shadrick Tucker - one negro girl Saray. Wit: Samuel Morgan, John Tucker, Absolom Tucker. S/ John Hood.

WB 5-472, 16 Apr 1789, wp 26 Apr 1798, will of John Hood, of Amelia Co.
Wife Catherine Hood - such maintenance as my executors think reasonable.
William Hood - 5 shillings sterling.
son Thomas Hood - 3 negroes Peter, Jack & Sam & that part of my land lying in the fork of the branch where he now lives.
dau Mary Hood - negro girl Nell & incr. & L30.
dau Fanny Tucker, wf of John Tucker - 5 shillings sterling.
dau. Rahab (Rachael?) Tucker, wf of Shadrack Tucker - 5 shillings sterling.
son Edward Hood, the whole of land where I now live, below the line already mentioned to son Thomas.
son Edward - remainder part of my est. be it of what nature or kind soever paying regard that if my son Edward should die without heir, his part be div. btwn his bro. Thomas & sister Mary, & if dau Mary die without heir, her part to go to her bro. Edward Hood.
Exor. Matthew Tucker, William Walthall, Millington Roach, Thomas Hood, Joseph Bevill & William Wilson.
Wit: Paschall Tucker, Elizabeth x Tucker Matthew x Tucker, Nancy x Reess(?).

WB 7-115. will of John Tucker, wd 6 Mar 1797, wp 26 Jul 1804, Leg: to Wife Martha - plantation where I now live - plus 3 negroes Dick, Luis, & Aggy, horses, hogs cattle, household & furniture & residue, for life or widowhood, & afterwards equally divided among my children Abel Tucker, my land (?), John Tucker, Shadrack Tucker, Ezekiahr Tucker. Ex: Absolom Tucker, Thomas Tucker, John Hood. Wit: Robert Tanner, Elam Tanner, Patsey Tanner.

WB 7-330, 8 Oct 1805, Rec 23 Jul 1807, I&A Est. of John Tucker. Included no slaves. Total value L63.7.2.

WB 7-331, 8 Oct 1805, Acct of Sale of Est. of John Tucker. 1.60.14.1 1/2.

PERSONAL TAX RECORDS

| 1782 | 1 | John | Tucker | |
|------|---|------|--------|------|
| 1786 | 1 | John | Tucker | Jun |
| 1787 | 1 | John | Tucker | Jun |
| 1788 | 1 | John | Tucker | Jun. |

*There were so many John Tuckers and John Tuckers Jr in Amelia Co., it is most difficult to distinguish between them, unless they can be identified by the land they owned. John Tucker, son of John & Martha, was not willed any land by his father, and there are no deeds for him in Amelia Co. However, if the above personal tax records pertain to the subject John Jr, then he was age 21 before or ca 1786, and was b before or ca 1765. A John Tucker of Amelia purchased land in Halifax Co.,Va: in 1785, and a John Tucker & wf Fanny of Prince Edward Co., Va. sold the same land in 1786*

HALIFAX CO., VA.

DB 13-341, 17 Nov 1785, rec 17 Nov 1785, Pleasant Shields of Halifax Co., to John Tucker of Amelia Co., for L51.5., 100 ac. on Tanfat (or Tawpot) Br. of Catawba Cr., bo. Solomon Stott(?), William Oliver, Hill, Thos Black. S/ Pleasant Shields. Wf Mary relinq dower right. *(See DB 14-293.)*

DB 14-293, 5 Sep 1787, rec 28 Jul 1788, John Tucker & wf Fanny of Prince Edward Co., to William Vasser, for L30., 100 ac. on Tanfat (or Tawpot) Br. S/ John x Tucker, Fanny x Tucker. Wit: Mel Spragins, John Crews, William Oliver, Elizabeth Barksdale, Sarah Wimbish. *(See DB 13-341.)*

John Tucker's brother, Shadrack, who married Fanny Hood's sister Rachael, also bought land in Halifax Co VA in 1793.

No deeds were found for this John Tucker in Prince Edward Co. Nothing more of this John Tucker is known by this compiler.

SUMMARY:

John Tucker, son of John Tucker & wf. Martha, b. c1765, m. c1786 Fanny Hood, dau of John Hood & wf Catharine of Amelia Co, probably in Amelia & Nottoway Counties, bought in 1785 and sold in 1787, land in Halifax Co, Va.

# T0112400a - SHADRICK TUCKER

## (or SHADRACK)
## MD RACHAEL HOOD
## SON OF JOHN TUCKER
## MD MARTHA _____

AMELIA CO. VA.

DB 18-44, 4 Aug 1786, John Hood to Shadrick Tucker, for love, good will & affection I have for Shadrick Tucker - one negro girl Saray. Wit: Samuel Morgan, John Tucker, Absolom Tucker. S/ John Hood.

DB 18-44. 4 Aug 1786, John Hood to John Tucker for love & good will & affection I have for John Tucker, one negro girl Amey. Wit: Samuel Morgan, John x Tucker, Abraham x Tucker. S/ John Hood. Rec 28 Dec 1786.

WB 5-472, 16 Apr 1789, wp 26 Apr 1798, will of John Hood, of Amelia Co.
Wife Catherine Hood - such maintenance as my executors think reasonable.
William Hood - 5 shillings sterling.
son Thomas Hood - 3 negroes Peter, Jack & Sam & that part of my land lying in the fork of the branch where he now lives.
dau Mary Hood - negro girl Nell & incr. & L30.
dau Fanny Tucker, wf of John Tucker- 5 shillings sterling.
dau. Rahab (Rachael?) Tucker, wf of Shadrack Tucker - 5 shillings sterling.
son Edward Hood, the whole of land where I now live, below the line already mentioned to son Thomas.
son Edward - remainder part of my est. be it of what nature or kind soever paying regard that if my son Edward should die without heir, his part be div. btwn his bro. Thomas & sister Mary., & if dau Mary die without heir, her part to go to her bro Edward Hood.
Exor. Matthew Tucker, William Walthall, Millington Roach, Thomas Hood, Joseph Bevill & William Wilson.

Wit: Paschall Tucker, Elizabeth x Tucker Matthew x Tucker, Nancy x Reess(?).

WB 7-115. will of John Tucker, wd 6 Mar 1797, wp 26 Jul 1804, Leg: to Wife Martha - plantation where I now live - plus 3 negroes Dick, Luis, & Aggy, horses, hogs, cattle, household & furniture & residue, for life or widowhood, & afterwards equally divided amony my children Abel Tucker, my land (?), John Tucker, Shadrack Tucker, Ezekiahr Tucker. Ex: Absolom Tucker, Thomas Tucker, John Hood. Wit: Robert Tanner, Elam Tanner, Patsey Tanner

WB 7-330, 8 Oct 1805, Rec 23 Jul 1807, I&A Est. of John Tucker. Included no slaves. Total value L63.7.2.

WB 7-331, Oct 8, 1805, Acct of Sale of Est. of John Tucker. L60.14.1 1/2.

PERSONAL TAX RECORDS

| | | | |
|---|---|---|---|
| 1782 | 1 | Shadrack | Tucker |
| 1787 | 1 | Shadrack | Tucker |
| 1788 | 1 | Shadrack | Tucker. |

*Shadrack Tucker was at least age 21 when listed on the Personal Tax Records in 1782, so he would have been born no later than 1761.*

*Shadrack Tucker did not own any land and did not appear on the Land Tax Records of Amelia Co.*

PRINCE EDWARD CO. VA.

DB 7-259, rec 16 Oct 1786, James Bauldwin & wf Lidda of Pr. Edward Co. to Shadrack Tucker of Amelia Co., for L170, 320 ac. in Pr. Edward Co., bo. Sandy Ri, John Brackett, John Clark, Thomas Clark. *(See DB 8-118.)*

DB 8-118, rec 18 Jun 1787, Shadrack Tucker & wf Rachael of Amelia Co. to John Rudd of Pr. Edward Co., for 5,000 lbs of not inspecterd tobacco, 320 ac. in Pr. Edward Co., bo. Sandy Ri, John Bracket, John Clark, Thomas Clark. S/ Shadrack x Tucker, Rachael x Tucker. At a court held 15 Dec 1794, Elizabeth wife of sd Shadrack relinquished her right of dower.

*(Note: Did wf Rachael die & did Shadrack marry wf Elizabeth, or is this an error in the court record?)*

*(See DB 7-259)*

No further record of Shadrack Tucker was found in Pr. Edward Co.

HALIFAX CO., VA.

DB 16-40, 26 Oct 1793, rec 23 Dec 1793, James Harris of Halifax Co. to 5hadrach Tucker of Amelia Co., for L90., 200 ac. in Halifax Co., bo. Jesse Strange on east, Richard Wade on south, William Ligon on west & Nathanial Vasser on north.

The Land Tax Records of Halifax Co. show that Shadrack Tucker held 220 ac. from 1794-1799.

Shadrack Tucker's brother John Tucker, who married Rachael Hood's sister Fanny, also bought and sold land in Halifax Co, VA.

This compiler has not further researched this Shadrack Tucker.

SUMMARY:

Shadrack Tucker, son of John Tucker & wf. Martha, b. ca. 1761 in Amelia Co., Va., md. Rachel Hood, dau. of John Hood & wf. Catherine, owned land in Pr. Edward Co. 1786-87, and in Halifax Co. 1793-1799.

# T0112500a - EZEKIAHR TUCKER

## (or HEZEKIAH)
## MD ANN TUCKER
## SON OF JOHN TUCKER
## MD MARTHA ____

AMELIA CO. VA.

MARRIAGE BOND

14 Mar 1787, Hezekiah Tucker md Ann Tucker, Security Sterling G. Thornton.

> *NOTE: The identity of Ann Tucker was not determined. She may have been Ann Tucker dau of William Tucker (ca 1720-1785) & wf Ann, named in Amelia Co. WB 3-300.*

WB 7-115. will of John Tucker, wd 6 Mar 1797, wp 26 Jul 1804, Leg: to Wife Martha - plantation where I now live - plus 3 negroes Dick, Luis, & Aggy, horses, hogs, cattle, household & furniture & residue, for life or widowhood, & afterwards equally divided among my children Abel Tucker, my land (?), John Tucker, Shadrack Tucker, Ezekiahr Tucker. Ex: Absolom Tucker, Thomas Tucker, John Hood. Wit: Robert Tanner, Elam Tanner, Patsey Tanner

WB 7-330, 8 Oct 1805, Rec 23 Jul 1807, I&A Est. of John Tucker. Included no slaves. Total value L63.7.2.

WB 7-331, Oct 8, 1805, Acct of Sale of Est. of John Tucker. L60.14.1 1/2.

PERSONAL TAX RECORDS

| 1785 | 1 | Hezekiah | Tucker |
|------|---|----------|--------|
| 1787 | 1 | Hezekiah | Tucker |
| 1788 | 1 | Hezekiah | Tucker |
| 1789 | 1 | Hezekiah | Tucker |
| 1790 | 1 | Hezekiah | Tucker. |

*Hezekiah Tucker was at least age 21 when listed on the Personal Tax Records of 1785, so he would have been born*

*before or ca 1764.*

*There is no record of his owning any land in Amelia Co.*

*This compiler has no further record of Hezekiah Tucker.*

SUMMARY:

Hezekiah Tucker, son of John Tucker & wf Martha, b. ca. 1764 in Amelia Co., Va., md. 1787 in Amelia Co., Ann Tucker.

# T0112100b - DANIEL TUCKER SR

## (1745-1824)

### OF MECHLENBERG CO., VA

*[In an early 1994 letter to a fellow Tucker researcher, B. DeRoy Beale stated "It was only recently that I concluded that the Daniel Tucker of Mecklenburg Co., VA. may be the son of John in the Francis Tucker line, and I have included that source data as well." The following chapter, with associated family line, is that source data. See chapter T0112100a and the associated family line for previous, 1986, thoughts Mr. Beale developed on this descendant.]*

MECHLENBERG CO., VA

DB 1-301, 18 Sep 1766, rec 16 Oct 1766, John Weatherford to Daniel Tucker, for L5., 20 ac., bo Wm. Johnson, John ___?, Phil Johnson. S/ John Weatherford.

> *Note: If Daniel Tucker was age 21 in 1766, he was born abt 1745. The above deed was the first one recorded in Mecklenburg Co., VA for Daniel Tucker, but it indicated that he was from Mecklenburg Co. His parents and siblings have not yet been identified.*

DB 5-244, 11 May 1778, rec 11 may 1778, Richard Hansford to Daniel Tucker, for L600.,325 ac., on great branch of Middle Bluestone Cr. bo. Ragsdale. S/ Richard Hansford.

DB 5-475, 13 Sep 1779, rec 13 Sep 1779, Daniel Tucker to Thomas Wilburn, for L100., 40 ac. on br. of Middle Bluestone (Cr.), bo Newsom, sd Wilburn, being part of land sd Tucker now lives on. S/ Daniel Tucker. Wit: Mark Moor, Jemima Moore, Samuel Moor. *(See DB 1-301, DB 5-244, DB 8-532.)*

> *NOTE: The above deed in 1779 did not include the relinquishment of dower by a wife. The deed below in 1780 was made by Daniel Tucker & wf Jane, but his marriage to Jincy (Jane) Cardin is not recorded until seven years later in 1787. Daniel Tucker was probably married twice, and his first wife probably died before 1787.*

DB 6-34, 8 May 1780, rec 8 May 1780, Daniel Tucker & wf Jane to Mathew Orsnbey, for L190., 55 ac., bo. Johnson, Bing, sd Ornsbey. S/ Daniel x Tucker. *(See DB 1-301, DB 5-244, DB 5-475.)*

> *NOTE: The above Daniel Tucker of Dinwiddie may not be the same Daniel Tucker of Mecklenburg. No record was found for the separate purchase of 277 ac.*

DB 6-510, 15 Jul 1785, rec 12 Sep 1785, Samuel Simmons & wf Elizabeth to Daniel Tucker, both of Mecklenburg Co., for L40.,100 ac., bo. John Berry(?), William Crutchfield, William Johnson, sd Tucker, Sampson Powers, William Holmes, George Farrow. S/ Samuel Simmons, Elizabeth x Simmons. Wit: Roger Gregory, Jno Simmons, Samson Power.

DB 8-532 13 Jul 1795, rec 13 Jul 1795, Daniel Tucker to Sampson Powers, for L20., 50 ac., being part of tract whereon Daniel Tucker now lives. bo John Stagalls, sd Powers, sd Tucker, Indian South Br. S/ Daniel Tucker.

DB 12-222 16 May 1805, rec 10 Jun 1805, John Simmons to Daniel Tucker Sr, for L60, 100 ac. bo Sampson Powers, James Bing, Daniel Tucker Jr, Richard Hill & sd John Simmons, it being part of land Simmons purchased of Samuel which lies west of the road leading from the house of sd Tucker to Mecklenburg courthouse., with 2 ac. lying on the opposite of the road. Wit: H. Terrell, John Tanner, Henry Hicks, John Holmes. *(See DB 12-333.)*

DB 12-323 Elizabeth Simmons, wf or John Simmons, rel right of dower to 100 ac. sold to Daniel Sr on 16 May 1805 *(See DB 12-222.)*

DB 13-173, William Insco, Daniel Tucker & Augustus Smith - Bond for William Insco appointed a Constable of Mecklenburg Co. for 2 yrs.

DB 14-552, Wiley Tucker, Daniel Tucker Sr, Dabney Phillips, & Thomas Johnson are bound for $1500.- Wiley Tucker is appointed a special constable to Matthew H. Davis for two years.

DB 15-274 , 18 Apr 1814, Wyllie Tucker, Daniel Tucker Sr., Jessee

Parish, bond to Wyllie Tucker appointed constable.

WB 10-96, wd 25 Feb 1824, rec 15 Nov 1824. will of Daniel Tucker Sr. of Mecklenburg Co.
Son Jesse Tucker - 5 shillings.
Son George Tucker - 5 shillings.
Son Daniel Tucker Jr - $20.
Son Tapley Tucker - 5 shillings.
Son Little B. Tucker - 5 shillings.
Son John Tucker - 5 shillings.-
Son James Tucker - 5 shillings.
Dau. Jane Tucker - 5 shillings.
Dau. Amy Tucker – 5 shillings
Wife Jane Tucker - residue of est until youngest dau. Charlotte Ann Tucker marrys or becomes of age, then my wife to have her third & bal to be sold & equally divided among my children not yet mentioned, & at wife's death, anything given to her be sold & equally divided among the same children., namely: Wiley Tucker, Alexander S. Tucker, Polly A. Tucker, Robert C. Tucker, Patsy E. Tucker, & Charlotte Ann Tucker.

Exors: wife Jane Tucker, Charles & William Baskerville. S/Daniel x Tucker Sr. Wit: Drury Lett, Samuel Simmons, Redmond x Smith, Jas. Hicks, Will B. Hill, Alfred Hansond.

*NOTE: The ancestry of this Daniel Tucker has not been identified by this compiler.*

WB 10-205, 19 Nov 1824, rec. 21 Feb 1825, I&A Est Daniel Tucker decd., incl negroes: Nancy(?) & young child Milly, Phillis & young child Grandesin(?), boy Lewis, girl Hannah, Elizabeth, Moses, & Betty. Total value $1,704.59. Apprs: John Hutcheson, James Johnson, W. V. Johnson, Sanford Bowers.

WB 12-91, rec 17 Nov 1828, Acct of Est of Daniel Tucker Sr.

WB 13-192, rec 19 Aub 1833, Acc of Est of Daniel Tucker Sr.

"Marriage Records, 1765-1810, Mecklenburg County, Virginia", collected & compiled by Katherine B. Elliott, South Hill, Virginia.

4 Dec 1788, Amy Tucker to Gardiner Crowder, Sur: David Crowder.

17 Jul 1787 Daniel Tucker & Jincy Cardin, Sur: George Stainback, Consent: John Cardin, father of Jincy.

8 Feb 1808, Daniel Tucker Jr & Mary Parrish, Sur: William Parrish.

23 Apr 1800, Gorge Tucker & Eddy Short, Sur: Daniel Tucker, Minister: Charles Ogburn.

6 Sep 1809, James Tucker & Jane Tucker, Sur: William Insco.

17 May 1810, James Tucker & Ruth Puckett, Sur: G. B. Hudson.

22 Jan 1793, John Tucker & Sally Nunnery, and 25 Jan 1793, Sur: Charnal Deardin, Minister: Charles Ogburn.

22 Dec 1797, Littleberry Tucker & Elizabeth Kelly, m 29 Dec 1797.

12 Nov 1787, Robert Tucker & Sarah Smith, Sur: Edward Elam.

9 Dec 1799, Tapla Tucker & Nancy Kelly, Sur: Daniel Tucker, Minister: William Creath.

DB 23-115, 12 Feb 1828, rec 18 Feb 1828. Robert C. Tucker, indebted to Waddy Jackson for $62.00, conveyed to Drury Let, his, interest in my father's est. (not named), consisting of negroes & land, horse, cow, furniture, etc.

DB 23-178, 7 Feb 1828. Alexander S. Tucker, indebted to Augustus Smith, sold to Robert C. Tucker, interest in my father's est. *(not named)*.

DB 23-520, 19 Jun 1829, rec 24 Jul 1829. Jane Tucker, indebted to Jesse Parrish & Augustus Smith for $170.00, sold to Churchwell Curtis, all her interest in the land whereon she now lives & all her interest in following slaves, Winny, Ma__s, Milly, Adderline. S/Jane x Tucker, Jesse x Parrish, Augustus x Smith.

*NOTE: Apparently Jane Tucker paid the debt, for she continued to hold 120 ac. until 1834.*

DB 26-415, 12 Oct 1835, rec 12 Oct 1835. Thomas A. Norvell & wf Charlotte, for $35.00, to Alexander Tucker, all their interest in land now in possession of Jesse Parish, which land was allotted to widow of Daniel Tucker Sr, in div. of his est., adj. Zachariah Curtis, est. of Zachariah Shackleford decd, Martha Bing & others; also a negro man Morris, which sd slave is also in possession of Jesse Parish & was allotted to widow of Daniel Tucker Sr as part of her dower. Charlotte A. Norvell, wf of Thomas A. Norvell, relinquish dower right.

*(Note: This must be Charlotte Ann Tucker, youngest dau of Daniel Tucker Sr, named in his will WB 10-96.)*

*Did Not Find Deed For Division Of Est Of Daniel Tucker Sr*

LAND TAX

1789-94 Daniel Tucker, 100 ac.
1796-1804 Daniel Tucker, 50 ac.
1805-15 Daniel Tucker, 150 ac. Saffolds Rd.
1816-24 Daniel Tucker Sr, 120 ac. Saffolds
1825-34 Jane Tucker, 120 ac. Saffolds Rd.

SUMMARY

Daniel Tucker, whose parents are not yet, identified, b c1745, d 1824, m 1st probably c1766 (wife not identified), m 2nd before 1780, but recorded 17 Dec 1787, Mecklenburg Co., VA, to Jincy (Jane) Cardin, dau of John Cardin.

It is believed this was his second marriage, since several of his children married shortly after this date.

It appears the children to whom he willed money, may be the children of his first wife, and the last named children to whom he willed the proceeds of sale of his estate, may be the children of his second wife Jane.

By first wife:

Amy Tucker, b c1767, m 1788 Gardiner Crowder.

Jesse Tucker, b c1772, m 1793 Nancy Carroll.

John Tucker, b c1772, m 1793 Sally Nunnery.

Littleberry Tucker, b c1776, m 1797 Elizabeth Kelly

Tapla Tucker, b c 1778, m 1799 Nancy Kelly.

George Tucker, b c 1779, m 1800 Eddy Short.

By second wife, Jane Cardin:

Wylie (Wiley) Tucker, b c1791, m 1812 Susanna Keaton.

Alexander S. Tucker m Elizabeth Bing.

Polly A. Tucker.

Robert C. Tucker.

Patsy E. Tucker.

Charlotte Ann Tucker m bef 1835 Thomas A. Norvell.

# T0112110b - AMY TUCKER

## (c1767-?)

## DAU OF DANIEL TUCKER SR

## (c1745-1824)

MECKLENBURG CO., VA

WB 10-96, wd 25 Feb 1824, rec 15 Nov 1824. will of Daniel Tucker Sr. of Mecklenburg Co.
Son Jesse Tucker - 5 shillings.
Son George Tucker - 5 shillings.
Son Daniel Tucker Jr - $20.
Son Tapley Tucker - 5 shillings.
Son Little B. Tucker - 5 shillings
Son John Tucker - 5 shillings.
Son James Tucker - 5 shillings.
Dau. Jane Tucker - 5 shillings.
Dau. Amy Tucker - 5 shillings.
Wife Jane Tucker - residue of est until youngest dau. Charlotte Ann Tucker marrys or becomes of age, then my wife to have her third & bal to be sold & equally divided among my children not yet mentioned, & at wife's death, anything given to her be sold & equally divided among the same children, namely: Wiley Tucker, Alexander S. Tucker, Polly A. Tucker, Robert C. Tucker, Patsey E. Tucker, & Charlotte Ann Tucker.
Exors: wife Jane Tucker, Charles & William Baskerville.
S/Daniel x Tucker Sr. Wit: Drury Lett, Samuel Simmons, Redmond x Smith, Jas. Hicks, Will B. Hill, Alfred Hansond.

"Marriage Records, 1765-1810, Mecklenburg County, Virginia", collected & compiled by Katherine B. Elliott, South Hill, Virginia.

4 Dec 1788, Amy Tucker to Gardiner Crowder, Sur: David Crowder.

*NOTE: If Amy Tucker was age 21 when she married in 1788, then she was b c1767, probably in Mecklenburg Co, VA, and probably was the oldest child of Daniel Tucker and his first wife.*

*NOTE: No further research was done on Amy Tucker. However, James Crowder m Elizabeth Tucker 12 Dec 1810 in Mecklenburg Co, VA., obviously there was another Tucker family living in Mechlenberg Co. at that time. This Elizabeth Tucker may be the sister of the unidentified James Tucker who married Jane Tucker in 1809. Also, Mrs. Audrey Stadler, in her letter of October 27, 1988, indicated that Archibald Tucker m 2nd Eliza Crowder 18 Apr 1849 in Fayette Co, WV.*

# T0112120b - JESSE TUCKER

## (c1772-?)

## SON OF DANIEL TUCKER SR

## (c1745-1824)

MECKLENBURG CO., VA

"Marriage Records, 1765-1810, Mecklenburg County, Virginia", collected & compiled by Katherine B. Elliott, South Hill, Virginia.

7 Nov 1793, Jesse Tucker & Nancy Carroll, Sur John Carroll.

*NOTE: If Jesse Tucker was age 21 when he married in 1793, then he was b c1772.*

DB 10-103, 1 Nov 1798, rec 10 Jun 1799, Jessey Tucker of Mecklenburg Co. to Battey Short, for L35., 71 ac. bo. Dennis Carrol, Thompson's Cr. Philip Reekes, Joseph Lett. S/ Jessey x Tucker, Wit.:Philip Reekes, Benjamin Reekes, Sally x Provise(?). *(See DB 10-160, which was recorded in 1797 prior to this deed.)*

DB 10-160, 9 Nov 1797, rec 11 Dec 1797, John Allen of Brunswick Co. to Jesse Tucker of Mecklenburg Co., for L10., 71 ac., bo. Thompson's Cr., Phill Reeker, Joseph Letts, Dennis Carrol. S/ John Allen, Wit: Philip Reeker, Benj. Reeker, Jno x Carroll, Dennis x Carroll. *(See DB 10-103, which was recorded in 1799 after this deed.)*

DB 10-255, 26 Apr 1800, rec 9 Jun 1800, George Tucker to Jessey Tucker, for L25., 69 ac. on_Latons bo. Elandges Old Rd., Mallet, Hutchison, Hanserd. S/ George x Tucker. Wit: Benjamin Reekers, Richard Crowder, Daniel x Tucker. *(See DB 13-175.)*

DB 13-175, 9 Feb 1807, rec 9 Feb 1807, Jesse Tucker to Pennington Sell for L60.12, 69 ac., on Laytons Cr, bo Hanserss(?), Eldridge old road, formerly William Maalletts, Hutcherson. S? Jesse x Tucker, wit: Peter Edwards, John Brown, Joseph Sell. *(See DB 10-255.)*

LAND TAX

1801-06 Jesse Tucker, 69 ac.

WB 10-96, wd 25 Feb 1824, rec 15 Nov 1824. will of Daniel Tucker
Sr. of Mecklenburg Co.
Son Jesse Tucker - 5 shillings.
Son George Tucker - 5 shillings.
Son Daniel Tucker Jr - $20.
Son Tapley Tucker - 5 shillings.
Son Little B. Tucker - 5 shillings.
Son John Tucker - 5 shillings.
Son James Tucker - 5 shillings.
Dau. Jane Tucker - 5 shillings.
Dau. Amy Tucker - 5 shillings.
Wife Jane Tucker - residue of est until youngest dau. Charlotte
Ann Tucker marrys or becomes of age, then my wife to have her
third & bal to be sold & equally divided among my children not
yet mentioned., & at wife's death, anything given to her be sold
& equally divided among the same children., namely: Wiley
Tucker, Alexander S. Tucker, Polly A. Tucker, Robert C. Tucker,
Patsey E. Tucker, & Charlotte Ann Tucker.
Exors: wife Jane Tucker, Charles & William Baskerville.
S/Daniel x Tucker Sr. Wit: Drury Lett, Samuel Simmons,
Redmond x Smith, Jas. Hicks, Will B. Hill, Alfred Hansond.

SUMMARY:

Jesse Tucker, son of Daniel Tucker Sr, b 1772, m 7 Nov 1793
Nancy Carroll.

Sold his land in Mechlenberg Co. in 1807.

# T0112130b - JOHN TUCKER

## (c1772-?)

## SON OF DANIEL TUCKER SR

## (c1745-1824)

MECKLENBURG CO., VA

22 Jan 1793, John Tucker & Sally Nunnery, and 25 Jan 1793, Sur: Charnal Deardin, Minister: Charles Ogburn.

*NOTE: If John Tucker was age 21 when he married in 1793, then he was b c1772.*

*NOTE: No deeds are recorded for this John Tucker in Mecklenburg Co., VA.*

WB 10-96, wd 25 Feb 1824, rec 15 Nov 1824. will of Daniel Tucker Sr. of Mecklenburg Co.
Son Jesse Tucker - 5 shillings.
Son George Tucker - 5 shillings.
Son Daniel Tucker Jr - $20.
Son Tapley Tucker - 5 shillings.
Son Little B. Tucker - 5 shillings.
Son John Tucker - 5 shillings.
Son James Tucker - 5 shillings.
Dau. Jane Tucker - 5 shillings.
Dau. Amy Tucker - 5 shillings.
Wife Jane Tucker - residue of est until youngest dau. Charlotte Ann Tucker marrys or becomes of age, then my wife to have her third & bal to be sold & equally divided among my children not yet mentioned., & at wife's death, anything given to her be sold & equally divided among the same children., namely: Wiley Tucker, Alexander S. Tucker, Polly A. Tucker, Robert C. Tucker, Patsey E. Tucker, & Charlotte Ann Tucker.
Exors: wife Jane Tucker, Charles & William Baskerville.
S/Daniel x Tucker Sr. Wit: Drury Lett, Samuel Simmons, Redmond x Smith, Jas. Hicks, Will B. Hill, Alfred Hansond.

SUMMARY:

John Tucker, son of Daniel Tucker Sr, b c1772, m 20 Jan 1793, Mecklenburg Co., VA, Sally Nunnery.

# T0112140b - LITTLEBERRY TUCKER

## (c1776-?)

## SON OF DANIEL TUCKER SR

## (c1745-1824)

MECKLENBURG CO., VA

"Marriage Records, 1765-1810, Mecklenburg County, Virginia", collected & compiled by Katherine B. Elliott, South Hill, Virginia

22 Dec 1797, Littleberry Tucker & Elizabeth Kelly, m 29 Dec 1797, Sur: John Tucker, Minister: Charles Ogburn.

*NOTE: If Littleberry Tucker was age 21 when he married in 1797, then he was b c1776.*

*NOTE: There were no deeds for Littleberry Tucker in Mecklenburg Co., VA.*

WB 10-96, wd 25 Feb 1824, rec 15 Nov 1824. will of Daniel Tucker Sr. of Mecklenburg Co.
Son Jesse Tucker - 5 shillings.
Son George Tucker - 5 shillings.
Son Daniel Tucker Jr - $20.
Son Tapley Tucker - 5 shillings.
Son Little B. Tucker - 5 shillings.
Son John Tucker - 5 shillings.
Son James Tucker - 5 shillings.
Dau. Jane Tucker - 5 shillings.
Dau. Amy Tucker - 5 shillings.
Wife Jane Tucker - residue of est until youngest dau. Charlotte Ann Tucker marrys or becomes of age, then my wife to have her third & bal to be sold & equally divided among my children not yet mentioned., & at wife's death, anything given to her be sold & equally divided among the same children., namely: Wiley Tucker, Alexander S. Tucker, Polly A. Tucker, Robert C. Tucker, Patsey E. Tucker, & Charlotte Ann Tucker.
Exors: wife Jane Tucker, Charles & William Baskerville.
S/Daniel x Tucker Sr. Wit: Drury Lett, Samuel Simmons, Redmond

x Smith, Jas. Hicks, Will B. Hill, Alfred Hansond.

SUMMARY: Littleberry Tucker, son of Daniel Tucker Sr, b c1776, m 22 Dec 1797, Mecklenburg Co., VA., Elizabeth Kelly.

# T0112150b - TAPLA TUCKER

## (c1778-?)

## SON OF DANIEL TUCKER SR

## (c1745-1824)

MECKLENBURG CO., VA

"Marriage Records, 1765-1810, Mecklenburg County, Virginia", collected & compiled by Katherine B. Elliott, South Hill, Virginia.

9 Dec 1799, Tapla Tucker & Nancy Kelly, Sur: Daniel Tucker, Minister: William Creath.

*NOTE: If Tapla Tucker was age 21 when he married in 1799, then he was b c1778.*

*NOTE: No deeds were found for Tapla Tucker in Mecklenburg Co., VA*

WB 10-96, wd 25 Feb 1824, rec 15 Nov 1824. will of Daniel Tucker Sr. of Mecklenburg Co.
Son Jesse Tucker - 5 shillings.
Son George Tucker - 5 shillings.
Son Daniel Tucker Jr - $20.
Son Tapley Tucker - 5 shillings.
Son Little B. Tucker - 5 shillings.
Son John Tucker - 5 shillings.
Son James Tucker - 5 shillings.
Dau. Jane Tucker - 5 shillings.
Dau. Amy Tucker - 5 shillings.
Wife Jane Tucker - residue of est until youngest dau. Charlotte Ann Tucker marrys or becomes of age, then my wife to have her third & bal to be sold & equally divided among my children not yet mentioned., & at wife's death, anything given to her be sold & equally divided among the same children., namely: Wiley Tucker, Alexander S. Tucker, Polly A. Tucker, Robert C. Tucker, Patsey E. Tucker, & Charlotte Ann Tucker.
Exors: wife Jane Tucker, Charles & William Baskerville.
S/Daniel x Tucker Sr. Wit: Drury Lett, Samuel Simmons, Redmond

x Smith, Jas. Hicks, Will B. Hill, Alfred Hansond.

SUMMARY:

Tapla (Tapley) Tucker, son of Daniel Tucker Sr & first wife (name unknown) b. c1778, m. 9 Dec 1799 Nancy Kelly.

# T0112160b - GEORGE TUCKER

## (1777-1847)

## SON OF DANIEL TUCKER SR

## (c1745-1824)

MECKLENBURG CO., VA

"Marriage Records, 1765-1810, Mecklenburg County, Virginia", collected & compiled by Katherine B. Elliott, South Hill, Virginia.

23 Apr 1800, George Tucker & Eddy Short, Sur: Daniel Tucker, Minister: Charles Ogburn.

DB 9-440, 12 May 1798, rec 11 Jun 1798, John Cardin to George Tucker, for $50., 50 ac., Richard Hutchison, Francis Kelly, William Mallet. S/ John Cardin. Wit: W. Baskervill, Edward Baskervill, Thomas Field, George Craghead. *(See DB 10-255 for 69 ac.)*

*NOTE: If George Tucker was age 21 when he bought land in 1798, he was b c1777.*

DB 10-255, 26 Apr 1800, rec 9 Jun 1800, George Tucker to Jessey Tucker, for L25., 69 ac. on Latons Cr., bo. Elandges Old Rd. Mallet, Hutchison, Hanserd. S/ George x Tucker. Wit: Benjamin Reekers, Richard Crowder, Daniel x Tucker. *(See DB 9-440 for 50 ac..)*

DB 11-283, 10 Nov 1802, Henry Ashton, Richard Hutcheson, James Bowing & Joseph Lett, commissioners appointed by court for sale of lands which John Short died seized, to George Tucker of Mecklenburg Co., for L58.4., 175 3/4 ac., bo. Freeman Short, Jacob Short, Fluds Br. Taylors Cr., Cornell, Taylor, Bradley, Jossie Oslin. S/ H Ashton, Richard x Hutcheson, James x Bowin, Joseph x Lett. Wit: William x Parrish, Daniel x Tucker Senr, Benjamin x Short.

DB 15-339, 3 Aug 1814, rec 6 Aug 1814. Goodwin L. Taylor & wf Nancy, for L75, to George Tucker, 125 ac. Taylor Cr., bo John Bentley, William Drumrigh, Askin, ,John Bradley,
*(See DB 15-340.)*

DB 15-340, 13 Aug 1814, Nancy Taylor, wf of Goodwin L. Taylor, relinquish right of dower to sale of 125 ac. to George Tucker. *(See DB 15-339.)*

DB 15-402, 15 Feb 1815, rec 20 Feb 1815, William Short & wf Rebecca, for L20, to George Tucker. 30 ac., bo James Hudgins, Isham David, Pennington, Taylor's road. S/William x Short, Rebecca x Short. Wit: Drury Pennington, George Steagall, Jno Bindord.

DB 16-9, 17 Aug 1815, rec 21 Aug 1815. George Tucker & wf Polly, for L125, to William Drumright, 125 ac. on b.s. Fox's Rd, bo Drumright, Thomas Taylor, John Bradley, est of Jesse Orline, S/George x Tucker. Wit: Thos Smith, Joseph Arnold, William Drumright.

DB 16-143, 24 Sep 1815, rec 19 Feb 1815, George Tucker & wf Polly, for $120., to Jesse Kirks, 30 ac. bo William Pennington, James Hudgins, Elizabeth Wall, Vaughan, x/ George x Tucker. Wit: George Stegall, E. B. Hudson, John Benf'd,

DB 16-229, 29 Dec 1815, Thomas Smith & wf Martha, for $207.50, to George Tucker, 163 ac., bo near house lately occupied by sd Smith & Blanton, John P. Smith, Zachariah Bugg, John Cook Jr, John Hall, John Wright

DB 17-124, 22 Aug 1817, rec 17 Nov 1817, John Hall & wf Caty, for 282? shillings, to George Tucker, 283 1/2 ac. bo Thomas Ladd, Crutchfield, Perginsons, Pennington, Mitchel's br. John Right. s/ John Hall, Catharine x Hall.

DB 18-48 2 Apr 1819, rec 21 Jun 1819, Berryman Farguson & wf Martha R., for $157.50, to George Tucker. 45 ac. bo Elizabeth Collins, Amos Hall, Taylor, Joseph Arnold, John P. Smith

DB 20-309, 24 May 1823, rec 5 Sep 1823. Jno. W. Gregory, Thomas Leggett & Benjamin P. Pennington, commissioners, for $165.00, to George Tucker, 189 ac., bo. Joseph Arnold, Robertson Ezell, Edmond Simmons. Wit: Isaac C. Walton, T. R. Cook.

WB 10-96, wd 25 Feb 1824, rec 15 Nov 1824. will Daniel Tucker Sr. of Mecklenburg Co.

Son Jesse Tucker - 5 shillings.

Son George Tucker - 5 shillings.

Son Daniel Tucker Jr - $20.

Son Tapley Tucker - 5 shillings.

Son Little B. Tucker - 5 shillings.

Son John Tucker - 5 shillings.

Son James Tucker - 5 shillings.

Dau. Jane Tucker - 5 shillings.

Dau. Amy Tucker - 5 shillings.

Wife Jane Tucker - residue of est until youngest dau. Charlotte Ann Tucker marrys or becomes of age, then my wife to have her third & bal to be sold & equally divided among my children not yet mentioned., & at wife's death, anything given to her be sold & equally divided among the same children., namely: Wiley Tucker, Alexander S. Tucker, Polly A. Tucker, Robert C. Tucker, Patsey E. Tucker, & Charlotte Ann Tucker.

Exors: wife Jane Tucker, Charles & William Baskerville.

S/Daniel x Tucker Sr. Wit: Drury Lett, Samuel Simmons, Redmond x Smith, Jas. Hicks, Will B. Hill, Alfred Hansond.

DB 28-60, 29 Feb 1837, rec 18 Oct 1838. George Tucker, for $1,100.00, to John W. Gregory, 175 ac., bo. James Smith, Pennington, S. Binford & others, & sd Geo. Tucker.

LAND TAX

| 1799 | George Tucker, 66 ac. |
|------|------------------------|
| 1801 | George Tucker, alienated |
| 1803-14 | George Tucker, 175 3/4 ac. on b.s. Taylors Cr. |
| 1815 | George Tucker, 336 3/4 ac. on b.s. Taylors Cr. |
| 1816 | George Tucker, 188 3/4 ac. |
| 1817 | George Tucker, 334 3/4 ac. on Taylors Cr. |
| 1818-19 | George Tucker, 628 1/4 ac. on Taylors Cr. |
| 1820-23 | George Tucker, 672 1/2 ac. on Taylors Cr. |
| 1824-25 | George Tucker, 672 1/2 + 189 ac. on Taylors Cr |
| 1826-36 | George Tucker, 672 1/2 + 198 ac. on Taylors Cr. |
| 1844 | George Tucker, 672 ac. on Taylors Cr. |

LAND TAX

1846-49    George Tucker, 674 ac. on Taylors Cr.
1850         George Tucker Est., 509 ac. On Taylors Cr.

WB 17-44, 23 Jun 1847, wp Jan court 1849. will of George Tucker
of Mecklenburg Co.
Wife Rebecca A. Tucker - one third of est both real & personal for
life.
Remainder of est to Thomas A. Norvell in Trust for sale & separate use
of my dau, Mary Ann Perkinsn life.
Exr: Thomas A. Norvell. S/ George x Tucker. Wit: E. Binford,
Michael Crutchfield, C. Drinaught.

SUMMARY:

George Tucker, son of Daniel Tucker Sr, b. c1777, m. 1$^{st}$ 23 Apr
1800 Mecklenburg Co., VA, Eddy Short, m. 2nd Rebecca, d 1847,
Mecklenberg Co., VA., and had issue:

      Mary Ann Tucker, m ____ Perkinson

# T0112170b - DANIEL TUCKER JR

## (c1782-?)

## SON OF DANIEL TUCKER SR

## (1745-1824)

MECKLENBURG CO., VA

"Marriage Records, 1765-1810, Mecklenburg County, Virginia", collected & compiled by Katherine B. Elliott, South Hill, Virginia.

8 Feb 1808, Daniel Tucker Jr & Mary Parrish, Sur: William Parrish.

DB 11-357, 2 Mar 1803, rec 123 Jun 1803, Joica Mollett & Martha Mollett the Daughter of Joica Mollett to Daniel Tucker Jr, for L34, 100 ac. bo. Daniel Tucker Sr, Powers, Be, ?, Richard Hutcheson, Jesse Tucker, , Newan Dortch, Simmons. S/ Joica x Mollett, Martha x Mollett. Wit: Joeeph McDaniel, Robvert McBean, Green Tucker, Daniel x Tucker Sr.

*NOTE: If Daniel Tucker Jr was age 21 when he bought land in 1803, he was born c1782.*

DB 15-470. 9 Apr 1815, rec 19 Jun 1815, Daniel Tucker Jr, & wf Mary, for $65.00, to Jesse Parrish 30 ac., bo Mary Hutcherson, Pennington Lett. S/ Daniel x Tucker, Mary x Tucker.

DB 19-222, 5 Aug 1821, rec 14 Sep 1821. By an indenture of trust 7 May 1820 btwn Daniel Tucker and me, Manual Dortch, that Daniel Tucker Jr conveyed 284 ac.. I, the sd Newman Dortch, declare that my name was only used in trust for Richard Apperson & I, sd Newman, in discharge of this trust & at request of sd Richard Apperson, have removed, release Daniel Tucker Jr. all of the estate. *(Note: The meaning of this is obscure.)*

DB 24-150 Daniel (Sr or Jr?) (failed to get this deed)

*NOTE: No more deeds were found through 1850 for Daniel Tucker Jr in Mecklenburg Co., although he still held 107 ac. through 1823 per land tax records.*

## LAND TAX

1804-19 Daniel Tucker Jr, 100 ac. Saffolds Rd.
1820-21 Daniel Tucker Jr, 242 ac. Pine Woods
1822-23 Daniel Tucker Jr, 107 ac. Pine Woods

WB 10-96, wd 25 Feb 1824, rec 15 Nov 1824. will of Daniel Tucker Sr. of Mecklenburg Co.
Son Daniel Tucker Jr - $20.
Son Tapley Tucker - 5 shillings.
Son Little B. Tucker - 5 shillings.
Son John Tucker - 5 shillings.
Son James Tucker - 5 shillings.
Dau. Jane Tucker - 5 shillings.
Dau. Amy Tucker - 5 shillings.
Wife Jane Tucker - residue of est until youngest dau. Charlotte Ann Tucker marrys or becomes of age, then my wife to have her third & bal to be sold & equally divided among my children not yet mentioned., & at wife's death, anything given to her be sold & equally divided among the same children., namely: Wiley Tucker, Alexander S. Tucker, Polly A. Tucker, Robert C. Tucker, Patsey E. Tucker, & Charlotte Ann Tucker.
Exors: wife Jane Tucker, Charles & William Baskerville.
S/ Daniel x Tucker Sr. Wit: Drury Lett, Samuel Simmons, Redmond x Smith, Jas. Hicks, Will B. Hill, Alfred Hansond.

## SUMMARY:

Daniel Tucker Jr, son of Daniel Tucker Sr., b. c1782, m. 1808, Mecklenburg Co., VA, Mary Parrish.

# T0112180b - JANE TUCKER

## (c1786-1850/60)

## DAU OF DANIEL TUCKER SR

## (c1745-1824)

## MD JAMES TUCKER

## (c1788-aft 1830)

MECKLENBURG CO., VA

WB 10-96, wd 25 Feb 1824, rec 15 Nov 1824. will of Daniel
Tucker Sr. of Mecklenburg Co.
Son Jesse Tucker - 5 shillings.
Son George Tucker - 5 shillings.
Son Daniel Tucker Jr - $20.
Son Tapley Tucker - 5 shillings.
Son Little B. Tucker - 5 shillings.
Son John Tucker - 5 shillings.
Son James Tucker - 5 shillings.
Dau. Jane Tucker - 5 shillings.
Dau. Amy Tucker - 5 shillings.
Wife Jane Tucker - residue of est until youngest dau. Charlotte
Ann Tucker marrys or becomes of age, then my wife to have her
third & bal to be sold & equally divided among my children not
yet mentioned., & at wife's death, anything given to her be sold
& equally divided among the same children., namely: Wiley
Tucker, Alexander S. Tucker, Polly A. Tucker, Robert C. Tucker,
atsey E. Tucker, & Charlotte Ann Tucker.
Exors: wife Jane Tucker, Charles & William Baskerville.
S/ Daniel x Tucker Sr. Wit: Drury Lett, Samuel Simmons,
Redmond x Smith, Jas. Hicks, Will B. Hill, Alfred Hansond.

"Marriage Records, 1765-1810, Mecklenburg County, Virginia",
collected & compiled by Katherine B. Elliott, South Hill, Virginia.

6 Sep 1809, James Tucker & Jane Tucker, Sur: William
Insco.

17 May 1810, James Tucker & Ruth Puckett, Sur: G. B. Hudson.

MARRIAGE RETURNS OF MINISTERS 1785-1854

22 _ 1824, James M. Tucker & Lucy R. Dortch

*NOTE: The identities of the James Tucker who married Jane Tucker in 1809, and the James Tucker who married Ruth Puckett in 1810, and the James M. Tucker who married Lucy R. Dortch in 1824 are not clear. Were they the same person? Was either of them the son of Daniel Tucker Sr, who willed 5 shillings to son James in his will 1824 (WB 10-96)? Was either of them the same James Tucker who died 1836 (WB 14-79)?*

*Note that G. B. Hudson was surety for the Tucker-Puckett marriage, and Charles Hudson was appraiser of the estate inventory and appraisement.*

No deeds were found in Mecklenburg Co. for any James Tucker during this period 1810-36. No James Tucker appeared on the Land Tax Records during this period 1810-36

See a separate chapter for the James Tucker who m Ruth Puckett and m Lucy Dortch, and who d 1836.

It is the conjecture of this compiler that Jane Tucker was daughter of Daniel Tucker Sr, and she married a James Tucker, whose identity is not yet determined. If the James Tucker and Jane Tucker were age 21 when they married in 1809, then they were b c1788. There were no deeds for that James and Jane Tucker in Mecklenburg Co., VA.

Mrs. Audrey Stadler advised in 1988, that James Tucker was included in the census (personal tax lists) of Mecklenburg Co. in 1810-1813; that James Tucker was included in the census (personal tax lists) of Botetourt Co 1814-1822 and that he and his wife were recorded in the 1820 census as ages 26-45. This would mean they were b btwn 1775-1794, and conforms with the estimated birth c1788 based on the marriage of James Tucker and Jane Tucker at age 21 in 1809 in Mecklenburg Co, VA.

Mrs. Stadler further advised that James Tucker d after 1830 in Kanawha Co, VA, and Jinsey (Jane) d 1850-6 in Fayette Co, WV, and that Jinsey was listed as age 64 in the 1850 census of Fayette Co, WV. This means she was b 1786, and also conforms with the estimated birth c1788.

My extensive research in the Virginia counties of Prince George, Amelia, Nottoway, Prince Edward, Brunswick, Lunenburg, Mecklenburg, Halifax, Pittsylvania, and Botetourt have not revealed any further information on the subject James Tucker and wife Jane Tucker. There were earlier James Tuckers in Mecklenburg Co, VA who are documented in my book "Tucker Trails Through Southside Virginia", but I have been unable to connect the subject James Tucker with any of them.

Many Daniel Tuckers are also documented in the above book, but I have not been able to identify the ancestors of Daniel Tucker of Mecklenburg Co.

SUMMARY:

James Tucker (parents not identified), b. c1786/8 probably in Mecklenburg Co, VA, d. aft. 1830 in Kanawha Co, VA, m. 1809, Mecklenburg Co, VA, Jane Tucker, b. c1786/8, d. 1850-69 in Fayette Co, WV, probably dau of Daniel Tucker (c1745-1824) of Mecklenburg Co, VA.

# T0112190b - JAMES TUCKER

## (c1789-1836)

## SON OF DANIEL TUCKER SR

## (c1745-1824)

MECKLENBURG CO., VA

"Marriage Records, 1765-1810, Mecklenburg County, Virginia", collected & compiled by Katherine B. Elliott, South Hill, Virginia.

6 Sep 1809, James Tucker & Jane Tucker, Sur: William Insco.

17 May 1810, James Tucker & Ruth Puckett, Sur: G. B. Hudson.

MARRIAGE RETURNS OF MINISTERS 1785-1854

22 ___ 1824, James M. Tucker & Lucy R. Dortch

*NOTE: The identities of the James Tucker who married Jane Tucker in 1809, and the James Tucker who married Ruth Puckett in 1810, and the James M. Tucker who married Lucy R. Dortch in 1824 are not clear. Were they the same person? Was either of them the son of Daniel Tucker Sr, who willed 5 shillings to son James in his will 1824 (WB 10-96)? Was either of them the same James Tucker who died 1836 (WB 14-279)? Note that G. B. Hudson was surety for the Tucker-Puckett marriage, and Charles Hudson was appraisor of the estate inventory and appraisement. No deeds were found in Mecklenburg Co. for any James Tucker during this period 1810-36. No James Tucker appeared on the Land Tax Records during this period 1810-36.*

It is the conjecture of this compiler that Jane Tucker was daughter of Daniel Tucker Sr, and she married a James Tucker, whose identity is not yet determined. There were no deeds for that James and Jane Tucker in Mecklenburg Co., VA.

82

It is also the conjecture of this compiler that the James Tucker who m. Ruth Puckett in 1810, and the James M. Tucker who m. Lucy R. Dortch in 1824, and the James Tucker named in the will of Daniel Tucker Sr in 1824 (WB 10-96), and the James Tucker whose estate inventory and appraisement was recorded in 1836 (WB 14-279), are all one and the same person.

No deeds were recorded for this James Tucker in Mecklenburg Co., VA. If that James Tucker was age 21 when he married in 1810, then he was b c1789.

WB 10-96, wd 25 Feb 1824, rec 15 Nov 1824. will of Daniel Tucker Sr. of Mecklenburg Co.
Son Jesse Tucker - 5 shillings.
Son George Tucker - 5 shillings.
Son Daniel Tucker Jr - $20.
Son Tapley Tucker - 5 shillings.
Son Little B. Tucker - 5 shillings.
Son John Tucker - 5 shillings.
Son James Tucker - 5 shillings.
Dau. Jane Tucker - 5 shillings.
Dau. Amy Tucker - 5 shillings.
Wife Jane Tucker - residue of est until youngest dau. Charlotte Ann Tucker marrys or becomes of age, then my wife to have her third & bal to be sold & equally divided among my children not yet mentioned., & at wife's death, anything given to her be sold & equally divided among the same children., namely: Wiley Tucker, Alexander S. Tucker, Polly A. Tucker, Robert C. Tucker, Patsey E. Tucker, & Charlotte Ann Tucker.
Exors: wife Jane Tucker, Charles & William Baskerville.
S/ Daniel x Tucker Sr. Wit: Drury Lett, Samuel Simmons, Redmond x Smith, Jas. Hicks, Will B. Hill, Alfred Hansond.

WB 14-279. 19 Oct 1836, I & A of Est of James Tucker, decd.. Included one negro woman Malinda & two children, Peggy & Hester. Total Value $1,175.00. Appraised by Charles Hudson, William Holloway & Chas W. Baird. Rec 15 Oct 1837.

DB 28-226, 5 Nov 1838, rec 15 Apr 1839. Jack H. Jones, for

$450., to Lucy R. Tucker, 125 ac. lying on Good's Ferry Rd, & bo. Lewis King, Rebecca J. Dortch, & others.

LAND TAX RECORDS

1844 - Tucker, Lucy R., 125 ac. Goods T. Road
1845 - Tucker, Lucy R., 125 ac. Alienated off to Lucy R. McDaniel

SUMMARY:

James Tucker, son of Daniel Tucker Sr, b. c1789, d. 1836, m. 1st 17 May 1810, Ruth Puckett, m. 2nd 22 ___ 1824, Lucy R. Dortch, all in Mecklenburg Co., VA.

# T01121100b - WYLIE TUCKER

## (c1791-?)

## (or WILEY)

## SON OF DANIEL TUCKER SR

## (c1745-1824)

MECKLENBURG CO., VA

MARRIAGE RETURNS OF MINISTERS 1785-1854

p 69, Tucker, Wylie & Susanna Keaton, 27 Jan 1812.

*NOTE: Wylie (Wiley) Tucker was most likely b c 1791, and age 21 when he married in 1812.*

DB 14-552, Wiley Tucker, Daniel Tucker Sr, Dabney Phillips, & Thomas Johnson are bound for $1500.- Wiley Tucker is appointed a special constable to Matthew H. Davis for two years.

DB 15-274 , 18 Apr 1814, Wyllie Tucker. Daniel Tucker Sr, Jessee Parish, bond to Wyllie Tucker appointed constable.

DB 17-420 17 Aug 1818, Wiley Tucker, Thomas Johnson, Daniel W. McDaniel, George Holins, bond for Wiley Tucker appointed constable.

DB 18-109, 20 Sep 1819, Wiley Tucker. Daniel M. McDaniel, Thomas Brame & Parish, bond for Wiley Tucker appointed constable.

DB 19-83 13 Nov 1820, rec 21 May 1821, Joseph Keeton & wf Martha, for $1.00, to Wiley Tucker, 50 ac., being a part of the land On which I now live, to be laid off where he the sd Wiley Tucker now lives, not taking any part of my plantation. Wit John Hutcherson, Jesse Parrish, Hundley Ragland.

WB 10-96, wd 25 Feb 1824, rec 15 Nov 1824. will of Daniel Tucker Sr. of Mecklenburg Co.
Son Jesse Tucker - 5 shillings.
Son George Tucker - 5 shillings.

Son Daniel Tucker Jr - $20.
Son Tapley Tucker - 5 shillings.
Son Little B. Tucker - 5 shillings.
Son John Tucker - 5 shillings.
Son James Tucker - 5 shillings.
Dau. Jane Tucker - 5 shillings.
Dau. Amy Tucker - 5 shillings.
Wife Jane Tucker - residue of est until youngest dau. Charlotte
Ann Tucker marrys or becomes of age, then my wife to have her
third & bal to be sold & equally divided among my children not
yet mentioned., & at wife's death, anything given to her be sold
& equally divided among the same children., namely: Wiley
Tucker, Alexander S. Tucker, Polly A. Tucker, Robert C. Tucker,
Patsey E. Tucker, & Charlotte Ann Tucker.
Exors: wife Jane Tucker, Charles & William Baskerville.
S/ Daniel x Tucker Sr. Wit: Drury Lett, Samuel Simmons,
Redmond x Smith, Jas. Hicks, Will B. Hill, Alfred Hansond.

DB 23-102, 5 Feb 1828, rec 8 Feb 1828. Trust. Whereas Wiley
Tucker is indebted to Churchwell Curtis for $30., and indebted to
Waddy J. Jackson, for $15.99, sold to Woodson V. Johnson his
interest in est. of Joseph Keeton, consisting of negroes, furniture,
etc.

LAND TAX

1822-26 Wylie Tucker, 50 ac. Buckhorn

SUMMARY:

Wylie (Wiley) Tucker, son of Daniel Tucker Sr & wf. Jane (Jincy)
Cardin, b. c1791 in Mecklenburg Co, VA, m. 27 Jan 1812 Susanna
Keaton (Keeton).

# T01121110b - ALEXANDER S. TUCKER

## (c1803-?)

## SON OF DANIEL TUCKER SR

## (c1745-1840)

MECKLENBURG CO., VA

WB 10-96, wd 25 Feb 1824, rec 15 Nov 1824. will of Daniel Tucker Sr. of Mecklenburg Co.
Son Jesse Tucker - 5 shillings.
Son George Tucker - 5 shillings.
Son Daniel Tucker Jr - $20.
Son Tapley Tucker - 5 shillings.
Son Little B. Tucker - 5 shillings.
Son John Tucker - 5 shillings.
Son James Tucker - 5 shillings.
Dau. Jane Tucker - 5 shillings.
Dau. Amy Tucker - 5 shillings.
Wife Jane Tucker - residue of est until youngest dau. Charlotte Ann Tucker marrys or becomes of age, then my wife to have her third & bal to be sold & equally divided among my children not yet mentioned., & at wife's death, anything given to her be sold & equally divided among the same children., namely: Wiley Tucker, Alexander S. Tucker, Polly A. Tucker, Robert C. Tucker, Patsey E. Tucker, & Charlotte Ann Tucker.
Exors: wife Jane Tucker, Charles & William Baskerville.
S/ Daniel x Tucker Sr. Wit: Drury Lett, Samuel Simmons, Redmond x Smith, Jas. Hicks, Will B. Hill, Alfred Hansond.

MARRIAGE RETURNS OF MINISTERS 1785-1854

 p 51 Tucker, Alexander S. & Elizabeth Bing 16 Sep (yr illegible)

WB 13-401, rec 16 Feb 1835. acct of Est of Robert C. Tucker by Alexander S. Tucker, Admr.

DB 21-77, 19 Feb 1824, rec. 19 Jul 1824. Daniel Daly & wf Polly, for 8,000 lbs of Petersburg imported crop tobacco, to Alexander S. Tucker, 129 ac., being the same land deeded fro Samuel Powers to sd Daniel Daly. *(See DB 27-28.)*

*NOTE: Alexander S. Tucker was most likely b c1803, and was age 21 when he bought land in 1824.*

DB 23-176, 21 Apr 1828, rec 21 Apr 1828. Alexander S. Tucker, indebted to Daniel T. Hicks, sold to Wm. B. Early, his interest, in right of his wf Elizabeth as heir, in est. of James Bing.

DB 23-178, 7 Feb 1828. Alexander S. Tucker, indebted to Augustus Smith, sold to Robert C. Tucker, interest in my father's est. (not named).

DB 26-147, 12 Sep 1834. John P. Smith, trustee, offered for sale Robert C. Tucker's interest in est. of his father Daniel Tucker Sr. decd, and Alexander B. Tucker became purchaser. (no. ac. not shown)

DB 26-415, 12 Oct 1835, rec 12 Oct 1835. Thomas A. Norvell & wf Charlotte, for $35.00, to Alexander Tucker, all their interest in land now in possession of Jesse Parish, which land was allotted to widow of Daniel Tucker Sr, in div. of his est., adj. Zachariah Curtis, est. of Zachariah Shackleford decd, Martha Bing & others; also a negro man Morris, which sd slave is also in possession of Jesse Parish & was allotted to widow of Daniel Tucker Sr as part of her dower. Charlotte A. Norwell, wf of Thomas A. Norwell, relinquish dower right.

*(Note: ac. not shown.)*

*(Note: This must be Charlotte Ann Tucker, youngest dau of Daniel Tucker Sr, named in his will WB 10-96.)*

DB 26-499, 13 Feb 1836, rec 13 Feb 1836. John G. Baptist, Clk of Mecklenburg Co. Court, exposed to public sale by Joseph A. Townes, deputy of Alexander S. Field, Sherrif of sd county, for arrears of tax, and Alexander Tucker became purchaser at price of 84 cents. 170 ac. *(See DB 27-41.)*

DB 26-500, 13 Feb 1836, rec 13 Feb 1836. John G. Baptist, Clk of

Mecklenburg Co, 123 ac. owned by William Wooten, was on --
Oct 1833, exposed to public sale by Joseph A. Townes, deputy of
Alexander S. Field Sherrif, for arrears of tax, & Alexander Tucker
became purchaser. for 85 cents. *(See DB 27-41.)*

DB 27-28, rec. 13 Aug 1836. Elexander Tucker & wf Elizabeth, for
$35.00, to George Bing, half the dower land of Daniel Tucker
decd.

DB 27-28, 12 Aug 1836, rec 19 Sep 1836. A. S. Tucker & wf
Elizabeth, for $150., to John Bing, 129 ac., being the land deeded
from Daniel Daly to A. S. Tucker. *(See DB 21-77.)*

DB 27-41 rec 17 Oct 1836. Alexander Tucker, about to move to the
west, appoint Isaac Holmes my lawful attorney, to rent out or to
make sale of 2 parcels of land, one 170 ac. & the other 123 ac.
   *(See DB 26-499, DB 26-500, DB 27-93.)*

DB 27-93, 25 Nov 1836, rec 17 Dec 1836. Isaac Holmes, P/A for
Alexander Tucker, to John P. Smith, 175 ac.
   *(See DB 27-41 for 170 ac..)*

LAND TAX

| | | | | |
|---|---|---|---|---|
| 1825-36 | Alexander S. Tucker, | 129 | ac. | Buckhorn - Dry Cr. |
| 1834-35 | Alexander S. Tucker, | 175 | ac. | Long Br. |
| 1834-36 | Alexander S. Tucker, | 82 | ac. | Eastland Cr. |
| 1834-36 | Alexander S. Tucker, | 74 | ac. | Taylor Cr. |
| 1835-36 | Alexander S. Tucker, | 170 | ac. | Flat Cr. |

BOTETOURT CO., VA

LAND GRANT

   G 105-311, 1 May 1851, Alexander Tucker, Botetourt Co,
   59 ac., br. entering Barbers Cr. n.w.

SUMMARY:

Alexander S. Tucker, son of Daniel Tucker Sr & wf. Jane (Jincy)
Cardin, b. c1824, Mecklenburg Co, VA, m. 16 Sep _____,
Mecklenburg Co., VA, Elizabeth Bing, dau of James Bing.

# T01121120b - ROBERT C. TUCKER

## (c1807-1835)

### SON OF DANIEL TUCKER SR

## (c1745-1824)

MECKLENBURG CO., VA

"Marriage Records, 1765-1810, Mecklenburg County, Virginia", collected & compiled by Katherine B. Elliott, South Hill, Virginia.

12 Nov 1787, Robert Tucker & Sarah Smith, Sur: Edward Elam.

*NOTE: If the Robert Tucker in the above marriage was age 21 when he married in 1787, then he was b c1766. However, this most probably is not the same person as Robert C. Tucker who appears to be one of the younger sons of Daniel Tucker Sr., by his second wife Jane Cardin.*

WB 10-96, wd 25 Feb 1824, rec 15 Nov 1824. will of Daniel Tucker Sr. of Mecklenburg Co.
Son Jesse Tucker - 5 shillings.
Son George Tucker - 5 shillings.
Son Daniel Tucker Jr - $20.
Son Tapley Tucker - 5 shillings.
Son Little B. Tucker - 5 shillings.
Son John Tucker - 5 shillings.
Son James Tucker - 5 shillings.
Dau. Jane Tucker - 5 shillings.
Dau. Amy Tucker - 5 shillings.
Wife Jane Tucker - residue of est until youngest dau. Charlotte Ann Tucker marrys or becomes of age, then my wife to have her third & bal to be sold & equally divided among my children not yet mentioned., & at wife's death, anything given to her be sold & equally divided among the same children., namely: Wiley Tucker, Alexander S. Tucker, Polly A. Tucker, Robert. C. Tucker, Patsey E. Tucker, & Charlotte Ann Tucker.
Exors: wife Jane Tucker, Charles & William Baskerville.
S/ Daniel x Tucker Sr. Wit: Drury Lett, Samuel Simmons,

Redmond x Smith, Jas. Hicks, Will B. Hill, Alfred Hansond.

DB 23-115, 12 Feb 1828, rec 18 Feb 1828. Robert C. Tucker, indebted to Waddy Jackson for $62.00, conveyed to Drury Let, his "interest in my father's est." (not named), consisting of negroes & land, horse, cow, furniture, etc.

> *NOTE: Robert C. Tucker was at least age 21 when he was party to the above deed in 1828, so he was b before 1807. Since no wife relinguished a dower right, he probably was not married.*

DB 23-178, 7 Feb 1828. Alexander S. Tucker, indebted to Augustus Smith, sold to Robert C. Tucker, interest in my father's est. *(not named)*.

DB 24-167 Robert C. *(failed to get this deed)*.

DB 26-147, 12 Sep 1834. John P. Smith, trustee, offered for sale Robert C. Tucker's interest in est. of his father Daniel Tucker Sr. decd, and Alexander B. Tucker became purchaser.

WB 13-401, rec 16 Feb 1835. Acct of Est of Robert C. Tucker, by Alexander S. Tucker, Admr.

SUMMARY:

Robert C. Tucker, son of Daniel Tucker Sr, b. bef 1807, d. 1835, probably unmarried.

# T01121130b - CHARLOTTE ANN TUCKER

## DAU OF DANIEL TUCKER SR

## (c1745-1824)

## MD THOMAS A. NORVELL

MECKLENBURG CO., VA

WB 10-96, wd 25 Feb 1824, rec 15 Nov 1824. will of Daniel Tucker Sr. of Mecklenburg Co.

Son Jesse Tucker - 5 shillings.

Son George Tucker - 5 shillings.

Son Daniel Tucker Jr - $20.

Son Tapley Tucker - 5 shillings.

Son Little B. Tucker - 5 shillings.

Son John Tucker - 5 shillings.

Son James Tucker - 5 shillings.

Dau. Jane Tucker - 5 shillings.

Dau. Amy Tucker - 5 shillings.

Wife Jane Tucker - residue of est until youngest dau. Charlotte Ann Tucker marrys or becomes of age, then my wife to have her third & bal to be sold & equally divided among my children not yet mentioned., & at wife's death, anything given to her be sold & equally divided among the same children., namely: Wiley Tucker, Alexander S. Tucker, Polly A. Tucker, Robert C. Tucker, Patsey E. Tucker, & Charlotte Ann Tucker.

Exors: wife Jane Tucker, Charles & William Baskerville.

S/ Daniel x Tucker Sr. Wit: Drury Lett, Samuel Simmons, Redmond x Smith, Jas. Hicks, Will B. Hill, Alfred Hansond.

DB 26-415, 12 Oct 1835, rec 12 Oct 1835. Thomas A. Norvell & wf Charlotte, for $35.00, to Alexander Tucker, all their interest in land now in possession of Jesse Parish, which land was allotted to widow of Daniel Tucker Sr, in div. of his est., adj. Zachariah Curtis, est. of Zachariah Shackleford decd, Martha Bing & others; also a negro man Morris, which sd slave is also in possession of Jesse Parish & was allotted to widow of Daniel Tucker Sr as part of her dower. Charlotte A. Norvell, wf of Thomas A. Norvell, relinquish dower right.

*NOTE: This must be Charlotte Ann Tucker, youngest dau of Daniel Tucker Sr, who had not "become of age" in 1824 when he named her in his will (WB 10-96). No marriage record was found.*

SUMMARY:

Charlotte Ann Tucker, dau of Daniel Tucker Sr & 2nd wf Jane (Jincy) Cardin, b bef 1824 in Mecklenburg Co., VA, m before 1835, Thomas A. Norvell.

# T0113000 - ABSOLOM TUCKER

## MD SUSANNAH _____

## SON OF FRANCIS TUCKER SR.

## MD ANN _____

AMELIA CO. VA.

LIST OF TITHABLES

1763-67 _ Absolom Tucker listed as 16-yr-up tithable in household of his father Francis Tucker Senr, therefore he was born ca 1747 & became age 21 ca 1768.

1769-70   1 Absolom Tucker

PERSONAL TAX RECORDS

1782-84   1   Absolom Tucker

1786-87   1   Absolom Tucker

1788   2   Absolom Tucker, Fr. Tucker

1789   3   Absolom Tucker, Fran. Tucker, Bos. Tucker

1790   3   Absolom Tucker, Era. Tucker, Bos. Tucker

1791   3   Absolom Tucker, Fra. Tucker, Bos. Tucker

*(See WB 8-210, 1815, Susannah Tucker)*

LAND TAX RECORDS - AMELIA CO.

1782-1815 Absolom Tucker, 200 ac. on Wintocomack Cr. adj. Richard Cardwell

1816       Absolom Tucker Est. 177 ac.

1816       Boswell Tucker 23 ac. deed from Absolom Tucker

1817-18    Boswell Tucker 69 ac. (*) on Wintocomack Cr. adj. George Cardwell

1817-18    Francis Tucker 76 ac. (*) on Wintocomack Cr. adj. Boswell Tucker

1817-18    Prudence Tucker 28 ac. (*) on Wintocomack Cr. adj. Francis Tucker

1817-18    Susannah Tucker 86 ac. (*) for life, on Wintocomack

Cr. adj. Thomas Barrett
*Note: (\*) 177 ac. of this land formerly belonged to Absolom Tucker Estate.*

LAND TAX RECORDS - LUNENBURG CO.

1791-1798 Absolom Tucker, 160 ac.

DB 13-158, 10 Nov 1774, Samuel Morgan Jun. & wf Mary, and John Morgan & wf Mary, to Absolom Tucker, for L125, 300 ac. on u.s. of Wintocomake Cr., bo. Wills' line, John Clancy's line. Wit: Peter Lamkin, Charles Irby, Wm. Crenshaw, Wm. Doswell. Rec. 27 Apr 1775. S/ Samuel Morgan, Mary Morgan, John Morgan, Mary Morgan. *(See DB 13-181.)*

DB 13-181, 20 Oct 1774, Francis Tucker Sen & Absolom Tucker & wf Susannah, to John Morgan, - for L25 & further consideration of 300 ac. in Raleigh Parish this day conveyed unto sd Absolom by sd John - 177 ac. l.s. Wintocomake Cr., being all the land which the sd Francis Tucker lately possessed & which he hath given to his son Absolom Tucker, bo. mouth of Horsepen Br. on Wintocomake Cr., Elias Witt's line, John Wilson's line, John Tucker's line, Abram Hood's line, Horsepen Br., Matthew Tucker's Sp. Br., a second br., Wit: Francis Tucker Jun., Simon Morgan, Edmd Wills. Rec. 27 Apr 1775. S/ Francis x Tucker Sen, Absolom x Tucker, Susannah x Tucker. *(See DB 13-158.)*

*NOTE: The above deed is confusing. The net result appears to be that Francis Tucker gave to his son Absolom Tucker 177 ac., for that is what Absolom held according to Land Tax Record.*

WB 2-207, will of Francis Tucker Sr. wd Jun 6, 1774, wp (date not shown).
Exec. Son Francis Tucker.
Leg: Grandson Francis Tucker - furniture.
Absolom Tucker - furniture.
Amy Hastains - bed.
Son Absolom Tucker - chairs.
Son Francis Tucker - negro Joe, all the rest of my estate.

Son John Tucker - one shilling sterling.

Dau. Prudence Coleman - one shilling sterling.

Dau. Pressillo Walker - one shilling sterling.

(no land was mentioned) (date recorded was not shown).

WB 2-218, Francis Tucker Est. I&A dated Feb 26, 1777 (date recorded not shown). Appr: George Worsham, Joseph Crowder & Henry Tucker. Adm. Francis Tucker. Value L78.15.9.

*(Note: From above Est I&A, it is assumed that Francis Tucker Sr. died in 1777. The grandson Francis Tucker is most probably son of the subject Absolom Tucker, since Absolom's brother Francis Jr did not have a son Francis.)*

DB 14-46, 7 Mar 1777, Mary Morgan to Absolom Tucker, for love & affection to son John Morgan, sold to Absolom Tucker, my part of the land he purchased of my son John Morgan (no bounds or acerage shown). Wit: Robt French, Robt Walthall, William Morgan. S/ Mary x Morgan. *(See DB 13-158.)*

*(Note: This seems to be a relinquishment of Mary Morgan's dower right.)*

DB 15-303, 20 Mar 1780, Absolom Tucker to Richard Cardwell, for L600., 60 ac. adj. Absolom Tucker & Eliza Wells. Wit: George Markan, Archer Traylor, John Tucker. S/ Absolom Tucker.

*NOTE: The origin of the above 60 ac. is not determined by this compiler.*

*NOTE: The following two deeds indicate that Absolom Tucker bought and sold land in Lunenburg Co, but continued to live in Amelia Co.*

LUNENBURG CO., VA.

DB 13-71, 6 Nov 1777, rec 18 Jan 1778, Edward Self of Lunenburg Co., to Absolom Tucker of Amelia Co., for L65., 168 3/4 ac., bo. Cockerham, Embry, Delgraftenreidt, Wood. Wit: Anthony Street, Churchill Gibson, William x Tucker. S/ Edward Self. Wf Jane relinq dower right. *(See DB 18-100 & DB 18-102A.)*

DB 18-100, 13 Feb 1799, rec 13 Feb 1799, Absolom Tucker & wf Susannah of Amelia Co., for L190, to Sharp Lamkin of Lunenburg Co., 168 3/4 ac. bo. Cockerham & Lamkin (formerly Embry), alGraffennid, McLurg (formerly Wood). *(See DB 13-71.)*

DB 18-102A, 11 Apr 1799, Susannah Tucker, wf of Absolom Tucker relinq dower right in 168 3/4 ac. conveyed to Sharp Lamkin.

AMELIA CO., VA.

WB 8-210, 21 Mar 1815, Susannah x Tucker relinquished the administration of estate of her deceased husband Absolom Tucker. Rec. 23 Mar 1815. Wit: Thos. T. Wills, Thos. Huddleston.

DB 24-206, 9 Jan ___ , rec 28 Mar 1816, Absolom Tucker of Lunenbur.g co, to Boswell Tucker of Amelia Co., for $115., 23 ac., bo. Richard Cardwell, John Broughton. S/ Absolom Tucker. Wit: Thos. T. Wills, Thomas Huddleston, Wm x Tucker.

*NOTE: The two transactions above are confusing. In Mar. 1815, wife Susannah relinquished estate administration of her deceased husband Absolom. Yet in Mar. 1816 a deed from Absolom to his son Boswell was recorded. It is most probable the deed was dated prior to, and recorded after, the death of Absolom. It reduced Absolom's land holdings from 200 ac. minus 23 ac. = 177 ac., which became his estate in 1816, as per land tax records. But more confusing is the fact that widow Susannah then held 86 ac. for life (which is 1/3 of 258 ac.), and 173 ac. fell to heirs: [Boswell (69 ac.), Francis (76 ac.), & Prudence (28 ac.)], plus Susannah's dower of 86 ac. = 259 ac. Land Tax Records further note that 177 ac. of this land was formerly Absolom Tucker's estate. This compiler is unable, to determine where the additional 82 ac. came from?*

*NOTE: There is recorded in Amelia Co. on 8 Dec. 1810 the marriage of Absalom Tucker to Polly Tucker, with Abel Tucker as Security, and on 14 Oct 1817 the marriage of Absolom Tucker to Adella Gilbert, with parent Zac Gilbert as Security. These two*

*Absolom Tuckers may be one and the same person, but neither is the same as the subject Absolom Tucker who was married to wife Susannah before 1772 and until he died 1815-16. Possibly Absolom Tucker & wf Susannah had a son Absolom b ca 1789, but this compiler has no proof of this.*

SUMMARY:

Absolom Tucker b ca 1747 in Amelia Co., the son of Francis Tucker Sr. & wife Ann. He was age 16 in 1763, age 21 in 1768, d ca 1816 in Amelia Co. He married Susannah before 1772, and had issue:

Francis Tucker b. ca. 1772.

Boswell Tucker b. ca. 1773, md. 23 Dec 1809 Judith Elam.

Prudence Tucker md. 27 Feb 1823 William Edmonds.

Absolom Tucker md. 1st 1810 Polly Tucker, md. 2nd 1817 Adella Gilbert.

# T0113100 - FRANCIS TUCKER

## SON OF ABSOLOM TUCKER

## MD SUSANNAH ____

## GRANDSON OF FRANCIS TUCKER SR

## MD ANN ____

AMELIA CO. VA.

WB 2-207, Will of Francis Tucker Sr., wd Jun 6, 1774, wp (date not shown).
Exec: Son Francis Tucker.
Leg: Grandson Francis Tucker - furniture.
Absolom Tucker - furniture.
Amy Hastains - bed.
Son Absolom Tucker - chairs.
Son Francis Tucker - negro Joe, all the rest of my estate.
Son John Tucker - one shilling sterling.
Dau. Prudence Coleman - one shilling sterling.
Dau. Pressillo Walker - one shilling sterling.
*(no land was mentioned) (date recorded was not shown).*

WB 2-218, Francis Tucker Est. I&A dated Feb 26, 1777 (date recorded not shown). Appr: George Worsham, Joseph Crowder & Henry Tucker. Adm. Francis Tucker. Value L78.15.9.

*(Note: From above Est I&A, it is assumed that Francis Tucker Sr died in 1777.)*

*NOTE: Francis Tucker Sr in WB 2-207, dated 6 Jun 1774, named "-my grandson Francis Tucker-". Francis Tucker Sr had three sons, Francis Jr. b 1723, John b 1726 & Absolom b 1747. Only Absolom had a son named Francis, who must be the subject "grandson Francis Tucker" referred to in the will of Francis Tucker Sr.*

## PERSONAL TAX RECORDS

| 1788 | 2 | Absolom Tucker, Fr. Tucker |
| 1789 | 3 | Absolom Tucker, Fran. Tucker, Bos. Tucker |
| 1790 | 3 | Absolom Tucker, Fra. Tucker, Bos. Tucker |
| 1791 | 3 | Absolom Tucker, Fra. Tucker, Bos. Tucker |

*(See WB 8-210, 1815, Susannah Tucker)*

## LAND TAX RECORDS

| 1782-1815 | Absolom Tucker, 200 ac. on Wintocomack Cr. adj. Richard Cardwell |
| 1816 | Absolom Tucker Est. 177 ac. |
| 1816 | Boswell Tucker 23 ac. deed from bsolom Tucker |
| 1816 | Francis Tucker 37 ac. deed from William Tucker |
| 1817-18 | Boswell Tucker 69 ac. (*) on Wintocomack Cr. adj. George Cardwell |
| 1817-18 | Francis Tucker 76 ac. (*) on Wintocomack Cr. adj. Boswell Tucker |
| 1817-18 | Prudence Tucker 28 ac. (*) on Wintocomack Cr. adj. Francis Tucker |
| 1817-18 | Susannah Tucker 86 ac. (*) for life, on Wintocomack Cr. Adj. Thomas Barrett. |

*Note: (*) 177 ac. of this land formerly belonged to Absolom Tucker Estate.*

The subject Francis Tucker was listed as a 16-yr-up tithable in the household of his father Absolom Tucker 1788-1791, Therefore he was born ca 1772, and attained age 21 ca 1793.

On the Land Tax Records of Amelia Co. a Francis Tucker held 37ac. in 1816, and 76 ac. 1817-1818 on Wintocomack Cr., which formerly belonged to Absolom Tucker Estate.

DB 24-84, 1815, Archer Coleman to secure debt to Francis Tucker, sold 75 ac. to Abraham Burton.

DB 24-191, 20 Jan 1816, rec 22 Feb 1816, William Tucker to Francis Tucker, for $211., 37 ac., bo. widow's dower line, Francis Tucker. S/ William x Tucker. Wit: Thomas T. Wills, Law Wills, William Booth.

> *NOTE: The identity of William Tucker is not clear. The name William does not appear anywhere else in the line of descent from Francis Tucker the Elder (ca 1663-1723). The 37 ac. was bounded by "widow's dower line", and Francis Tucker, but the name of the widow was not shown. In 1815, Abel Tucker, son of John & Martha, sold 195 ac. to William Tucker. It would appear from the Land Tax Records that this 37 ac. is part of the 195 ac., for the Land Tax acerage was reduced to 158 ac. But in 1818, the Land Tax Record was corrected back to 196 ac. This would imply that the 37 ac. came from some other source, possibly an inheritance, since there is no deed. There is recorded in Amelia Co. on 22 Jun 1810, the marriage of William Tucker to Sally Tucker, and on 8 Dec 1810 the marriage of Absolom Tucker to Polly Tucker, with Abel Tucker as. Security for both marriages.*

DB 27-302, 24 May 1825, rec 26 May 1825, Francis Tucker to William Edmunds & James Edmund, for $452., 113 ac., bo. Thomas Barretts, est of Wm. Booth, Cardwell, sd Wm. Edmunds, Boswell Tucker. S/ Francis x Tucker. Wit: John Mills, John Clay, William x Tucker.

> *(See DB 24-191 for 37 ac. from William Tucker, plus Land Tax Record for 76 ac. inherited from father Absolom Tucker.)*

DB 27-566, 16 Sep 1826, rec 28 Sep 1826, John O. Tanner & wf Ann to Frances Tucker for $650., 132 ac., bo. William Wills, Ludy Tanner, Henry H. Southall, Joel Mann, Dumplin branch, William Wells. *(See DB 31-53.)*

DB 31-53, 29 Aug 1832, Francis Tucker to William Edmunds for $650., 132 ac., bo. Wm. Wills, Lucy Tanner, Henry W. Southall, Jack Mann, Dumplin Br. S/ Francis x Tucker. Wit: John Wills,

James x Edmunds, Wm x Wills. *(See DB 27-566.)*

*NOTE: William Edmunds in above two deeds is brother-in-law of Francis Tucker, having married his sister Prudence.*

SUMMARY:

Francis Tucker, son of Absolom Tucker & wf Susannah, b ca 1772 in Amelia Co., Va. No marriage record could be found for him in Amelia Co., and none of his deeds mentioned a wife. He sold his land in Amelia Co. in 1832, and no further deeds were recorded for him.

# T0113200 - BOSWELL TUCKER

## MD JUDITH ELAM
## SON OF ABSOLOM TUCKER
## MD SUSANNAH _____

AMELIA CO. VA.

PERSONAL TAX RECORDS

1788  2  Absolom Tucker, Fr. Tucker

1789  3  Absolom Tucker, Fran. Tucker, Bos. Tucker

1790  3  Absolom Tucker, Fra. Tucker, Bos. Tucker

1791  3  Absolom Tucker, Fra. Tucker, Bos. Tucker

*(See WB 8-210, 1815, Susannah Tucker.)*

Boswell Tucker was listed as a 16-yr-up tithable in the household of his father Absolom Tucker beginning in 1789, therefore he was born ca 1773, and age 21 ca 1794.

LAND TAX RECORDS

| | | | |
|---|---|---|---|
| 1782-1815 | Absolom Tucker | 200 ac. | on Wintocomack Cr. adj. Richard Cardwell |
| 1816 | Absolom Tucker Est. | 177 ac. | |
| 1816 | Boswell Tucker | 23 ac. | deed from Absolom Tucker |
| 1817-18 | Boswell Tucker | 69 ac. | (*) on Wintocomack Cr adj. George Cardwell |
| 1817-18 | Francis Tucker. | 76 ac | (*) on Wintocomack Cr. adj. Boswell Tucker |
| 1817-18 | Prudence Tucker | 28 ac. | (*) on Wintocomack Cr. adj. Francis Tucker |
| 1817-18 | Susannah Tucker | 86 ac. | (*) for life, on Wintocomack Cr. Adj Thomas Barrett. |

*Note: (*) 177 ac. of this land formerly belonged to Absolom Tucker Estate.*

MARRIAGE BOND

23 Dec 1809, Boswell Tucker md Judith Elam, Sec. Abram Powell.

DB 23-253, 19 Sep 1810, rec 29 Sep 1810, Thos T. Wills to secure debt to Boswell Tucker, sold slaves.

DB 23-600, 28 Dec 1812, rec 22 Apr 1813, William Nance to Boswell Tucker, for $60., 2 ac. (no bounds given). *(See 24-438.)*

WB 8-210, 21 Mar 1815, Susannah x Tucker relinquished the administration of estate of her deceased husband Absolom Tucker. Rec. 23 Mar 1815. Wit: Thos. T. Wills, Thos. Huddleston.

DB 24-206, 9 Jan rec 28 Mar 1816, Absolom Tucker of Lunenburg Co. to Boswell Tucker of Amelia Co., for $115, 23 ac., Richard Cardwell, John Broughton. S/ Absolom Tucker. Wit: Thos. T. Wills, Thomas Huddleston, Wm x Tucker. *(See 08 24-321.)*

> *NOTE: Although the dates are confusing, Boswell Tucker's father Absolom, apparently died ca 1815-16.*

DB 24-321, 21 Aug 1816, rec 28 Nov 1816, John Broughton & wf Elizabeth to Boswell Tucker, for $161, 23 ac. on Wintopomake Cr. adj. sd. Boswell Tucker. *(See DB 24-206.)*

DB 24-438, 10 May 1817, rec 22 May 1817, Boswel Tucker & wf Judith to Abraham A. Powell, for $80., 2 ac., adj Abraham A. Powell & est of Robert James decd. S/ Boswell x Tucker, Judith x Tucker. *(See DB 23-600.)*

DB 25-553, 20 Jan 1821, rec 22 Mar 1821, Abel Powell to Boswell Tucker, for L36., furniture, household furnishings, hogs, & corn, etc. S/ Abel Powell, Thos T. Wills, Moses Mitchell, W. T. Green.

DB 26-246, 7 Jun 1823, rec 28 Aug 1823, William Edmonds & wf Prudence to Boswell Tucker, for $51.33., 14 2/3 ac., being my part of my mother's dower land, bo. Frances Tucker, sd Boswell Tucker.

*NOTE: Prudence Edmonds was Boswell Tucker's sister.*

DB 30-293, 22 Oct 1831, rec 24 Nov 1831, Boswell Tucker to Thomas Barrett, for $49., 7 3/8 ac. on w.s. Wintocomake Cr. near head of the mill pond which sd Barrett purchased for the purpose of obtaining a good road around sd pond. *(See DB 30-294.)*

DB 30-294, 22 Oct 1831, rec 21 Nov 1831, Thomas Barrett & wf Ermine J. to Boswell Tucker, for $40., 7 3/8 ac. bo. Bowles, Barrett, Edmunds, sd Tucker. *(See DB 30-293.)*

DB 35-13, 9 Dec 1841, rec 29 Jan 1842, Boswell Tucker to Thomas Barrett for $500., 118 ac. bo. James & William Edmunds, George Booth, sd Thomas Barrett, est. of Henry Bowles.

*NOTE: The source of the above 118 ac. is not clear. This Boswell Tucker was not further researched.*

SUMMARY:

Boswell Tucker born ca 1773 in Amelia Co., Va., son of Absolom Tucker & wf Susannah, married 1809 in Amelia Co., Judith Elam.

# T0120000 - JOHN TUCKER SR

## MD (ANN TALLY?)
## SON OF FRANCIS TUCKER THE ELDER
## MD MARY ____

PRINCE GEORGE CO. VA. [1]

p 750, Survey, 8 May 1712, John Tucker, 200 ac., on Nummiseen Cr., called Ellington's Br., Pr. Geo. Co. *(See Patent 10-338.)*

*NOTE: If this John Tucker was age 21 when he surveyed land in 1712, then he was b c1691 most probably in Charles City Co.*

p 1105, 8 Jan 1727. Godfrey Ragsdale of Bristol Parish, Henrico Co., to Benjamin Ragsdale of same parish, Pr. Geo. Co., 160 ac. at Namosend in Bristol Parish, Pr. Geo. Co., bo. John Tuckers line, John Ellington's line, sd Benjamin Ragsdale's spring branch, Henry Cox's line; being one moiety of a tract of 320 ac. taken up by sd Godfrey Ragsdale.

Wills, p 158, 14 May 1717, Accts. of Est. of James Boreman, decd., mentions Thos. Scarbrough, John Tucker & others.

Will, p663, Will of Francis Tucker of Bristol Parish, d 12 Dec 1722, p 10 Dec 1723.
son Francis, land on n.e. side of Mawhipponoak Cr. lower end.
son John, land n.s. same creek, joining Henry Mayes.
son Henry, land bet. sons Francis & John, inc. plantation where I now live.
son Abram, land n.s. Mawhipponoak Cr. joining son Henry & Thomas Mitchell.
son Mathew, land joining Thomas Mitchell.
All goods to be equally divided bet. children & wife Mary.
Wit: Mathew Mayes, Henry Mayes, John Powell. S/ Francis x Tucker.

*NOTE: The lands on Mawhipponoak Cr., which Francis Tucker the Elder willed to his sons, lay in the area which was separated from Prince George Co. in 1752 to form Dinwiddie Co, and only fragmented records remain for either county.*

Fragment p 915, Aug 9, 1726. Inv. of certin particulars of Francis Tucker's est. by Francis (T) Tucker, Adm'r.

Deed. p671, 13 Jan 1723, John Tucker Jr(?), of Pr. Geo. Co., to Patrick Dorcum, 100 ac. where sd John Tucker lately lived on w.s. of Mawhipponoak Cr. next to Henry Mayes. S/ John (I) Tucker. Wit: Wm. Cureton, William Short, Jos. (IR) Renn. Rec. Jan 14, 1723. Ann, wife of John Tucker, ack. dower int. *(See Patent 11-77 & Will p663.)*

> *NOTE: Francis Tucker the Elder, in 1723, willed to his son John, land next to Henry Mayes. John Tucker patented land in 1721 adj to Henry Mayes. John Tucker & wf Ann sold land in 1723 next to Henry Mayes. This proves that the John Tucker who married Ann was the son of Francis Tucker the Elder.*

Wills, p 1016, 13 Jun 1727, Inv. of John Tucker by John (I) Tally, adm'r. Appr. by John Cordle, Robert Tucker, William (WC) Coleman.

> *NOTE: John Tucker apparently d intestate in 1727 in Prince George Co.. Administrator John Tally was most probably his brother-in-law. (See Amelia Co. WB 1-10.)*

PATENTS [2]

Patent 10-338, John Tucker, 15 Jul 1717, Pr. Geo. Co., 200 ac., e.s. Namusond Cr., beg. e.s. Ellington's Br. (Dinwiddie Co. was formed from this area of Pr. Geo. Co. in 1752).

Patent 11-77, John Tucker, 13 Nov 1721, Pr. Geo. Co., 100 ac., w.s. Mawhipponeck Cr., adj. Henry Mays. *(See Deed p 671.)*

> *NOTE: See Deed p 671 and also Will p 663 of Francis Tucker in which he willed to son John, land on w.s. Mawhipponoak Cr. adj. Henry Mays. This is indication that subject John Tucker is son of Francis Tucker the Elder who d 1723 & wf Mary.*

# BRISTOL PARISH REGISTER [3]

Sara dau of John & Ann Tucker born 12th Janr last bapt May 13th 1722.

John son of John & Anne Tucker born 9th Septr last bap 6th Nov 1724.

_____ Dat (daughter) of Jno and Anne Tucker born ____.

francis Son of John and Ann tucker born 3d Janr 1726.

## AMELIA CO. VA.

1735, Amelia Co. was formed from Pr. Geo. Co., west and north of Namozine Cr.

WB 1-10, wd 23 May 1726, wp 21 Nov 1740, will of John Tally of Bristol Parish, Pr. Geo. Co., Va.
Exr: wife Anna.
son John - land up. cor. of Allen Howard to the Cattale ss Cattale.
son Henery - Beach 8r. Rocky Run & s.s. Deep Cr.
son Lodowick - Namaseen Cr. to River.
son William - s.s. Back Meadow Run, Thos. Hood's line to line of John Tally.
son Allen - land where chapel stands.
son Abram - where I live at wife's death.
grandson John Tucker - 100 ac. s.s. Deep Cr., joining my grandson John Powell.
grandson John Powell to have first choice, son Lodwick to have remainder land s.s. Deep Cr. after two grandsons make their choice.
dau. Sibella Tally.
dau. Ruth Tally.
dau. Mary Powell.
wife Anna - land & plantation where I live for her natural life, also all pers. est. & at her decease, land & plant. to Abram & pers. est. to be divided among all my children.
Wit: Seth More, Richard x Tally, Philip x Dunevant.

WB 1-10, 20 Feb 1740, John Tally I&A. Appr: George Tucker, Robert Cusons, Robert Tucker. Admr: William Talley.

DB 1-530. 17 Jul 1741, Bond. John Tucker, Jr., orphan of John

Tucker, has chosen John Waller as his guardian. Sec. William Traylor. L100. (ca age 17)

DB 1-530. 17 Jul 1741, Bond. Sarah Tucker, orphan of John Tucker, decd, has chosen William Traylor to be her guardian. Sec. John Waller. L100. (ca age 19)

DB 1-531, 17 Jul 1741, Bond. Francis Tucker, orphan of John Tucker, has chosen William Traylor as his guardian. Sec. John Waller. L100. (ca age 15)

ASSUMPTIONS AND CONCLUSIONS:

John Tucker, son of Francis Tucker the Elder & wife Mary, b ca 1691 in Charles City Co., d 1727 in Pr. George Co., married ca 1721 Ann Talley, dau. of John Talley & wf Ann (Anna), and had issue:

Sarah Tucker b 1722

John Tucker Jr b 1724

Francis Tucker b 1726

a daughter no name and date given.

John Tucker's wife, Ann Talley, died probably in 1726, and her father, John Talley did not mention her in his will written in 1726, but rather left land to his grandson John Tucker.

*(See Amelia Co. WB 1-10, will of John Talley of Bristol Parish, Pr. Geo. Co. written in 1726, and probated in 1740 in Amelia Co.).*

John Tucker, widower of Ann Talley, died in 1727, and John Talley was administrator of his estate.. *(See Wills p 1016 above.)*

The orphan children of John & Ann Tucker were probably taken into the home of their grandparents John & Anna Talley.

The grandfather John Talley died in 1740. *(See WB 1-10 as above.)*

The orphan children of John & Ann Tucker, namely, John Tucker Jr., Sarah Tucker and Francis Tucker, then chose their guardians in 1741. *(See Amelia Co. DB 1-530 and 1-531 above.)*

See separate chapters for sons John Tucker Jr and Francis Tucker.

1. Weisiger, Benjamin B, III, "Prince George County, Virginia Wills & Deeds 1713-1728", 1973
2. Card File of Land Patents and Grants, Virginia State Library Archives
3. Boddie, John B., "Births 1720-1792 from the Bristol Parishs Register for Henrico, Prince George and Dinwiddie."

# T0121000 - JOHN TUCKER JR

## MD BLANCH _____
### SON OF JOHN TUCKER SR
### MD ANN TALLEY

BRISTOL PARISH REGISTER [1]

John son of John & Ann Tucker born 9th Septr last bap 6th Nov 1724.

PRINCE GEORGE CO. VA. [2]

p 1016, Wills, 13 Jun 1727, Inv. of John Tucker by John (I) Tally, Admsr. Appr. by John Cordle, Robert Tucker, William (WC) Coleman.

> *NOTE: This is the inventory of John Tucker Sr, who died intestate, leaving orphan children Sarah Tucker b 1722, John Tucker Jr b 1724, and Francis Tucker b 1726. See previous chapter for John Tucker Sr and Ann Tally.*

-7

PATENT [3]

Patent 22-522, 20 Sep 1745, John Tucker, Pr. Geo Co., 252 ac 1.s. Beaverpond Cr., adj. Robert Tucker & Langford.

> *NOTE: This compiler believes this patent belongs to the subject John Tucker Jr, who was b 1724 and became age 21 in 1745.*

> *NOTE: There is a Patent, 13-270, 13 Oct 1727 for Robert Tucker (Sr), Pr. Geo. Co. 331 ac. by a Gr. Br. against the Beaver Pond. Robert Tucker Sr then sold to his sons Robert Tucker Jr and John Tucker, 165 1/2 ac. each (half of 331 ac.) by a Gr. Br. against the Beaver Pond, which deeds were recorded in Amelia Co. DB 1-341 and 1-344, 10 Oct 1741. Citations were found for disposing of those lands. No deed could be found for disposing of the subject 252 ac. patented in 1745, either by the subject John Jr son of John Sr, or by the other John son of Robert Sr. However, see Amelia Co. DB 17-378 below which probably pertains to 200 ac. of this 252 ac.*

AMELIA CO. VA.

1735, Amelia Co was formed from Pr. Geo Co., west and north of Namozine Cr.

WB 1-10, wd 23 May 1726, wp 21 Nov 1740, will of John Tally of Bristol Parish, Pr. Geo. Co., Va.
Exr: wife Anna.
son John - land up. cor. of Allen Howard to the Cattale ss Cattale.
son Henery - Beach Br. Rocky Run & s.s. Deep Cr.
son Lodowick - Namaseen Cr. to River.
son William - s.s. Back Meadow Run, Thos. Hood's line to line of John Tally.
son Allen - land where chapel stands.
son Abram - where I live at wife's death.
grandson John Tucker - 100 ac. s.s. Deep Cr., joining my grandson John Powell.
grandson John Powell to have first choice, son Lodwick to have remainder land s.s. Deep Cr. after two grandsons make their choice.
dau. Sibella Tally. Co
dau. Ruth Tally
dau. Mary Powell.
wife Anna - land & plantation where I live for her natural life, also all pers. est. & at her decease, land & plant. to Abram & pers. est. to be divided among all my children.
Wit: Seth More˙, Richard x Tally, Philip x Dunevant.

WB 1-10, 20 Feb 1740, John Tally I&A. Appr: George Tucker, Robert Cusons, Robert Tucker. Admr: William Talley.

*NOTE: The grandson John Tucker is believed to be the subject John Tucker Jr, orphaned son of John Tucker Sr who married Ann Tally, dau of John Tally Sr & wf Anna.*

DB 1-530, 17 Jul 1741, Bond, John Tucker Jr., orphan of John Tucker, has chosen John Waller as his guardian. Sec. William Traylor. L100. *(Note: John Tucker Jr was age 16 at time of this guardianship.)*

DB 2-254, d 20 Feb 1745, John Waller to John Tucker for L60.,

200 ac. bo. Abraham Green's line & cor., Childs' line, being land Pat. to sd Waller on Sep 22, 1739. Rec. Feb 22, 1745. Wife Ann relinq. dower. *(See DB 2-438.)*

DB 2-438. 22 Sep 1746, John Tucker to Abraham Green for L30., 200 ac. bo. lines of Green, Childs & John Powell, Green's cor. & line, being a Pat. to John Waller on Sep 22, 1739, & by him conveyed to John Tucker. Wit: John Powell, Mary x Powell, William Crawley, Thomas Bevill. Wife Blanch rel dower. *(See DB 2-254 above.)*

DB 5-112. 23 Nov 1753, Joseph Ragsdale of Lunenburg Co. to Jhn (John) Tucker of Amelia Co., for L47., 196 ac. in ridge btwn Wintocomake Cr. & Sweathouse Cr. & on b.s. of road adj. Bevill's, Newman's, bo. Bevills's cor, Newman's cor. & line. Wit: Edward Tanner, Edward Bevill, John Powell. *(See DB 6-443 below.)*

DB 6-433, 15 Feb 1759, John Tucker & wf Blanch to Edward Tanner, for L35., 196 ac. bo. my own corner, Daniel Coleman's line, Burton's line. Wit: Peter Burton, Jeremiah Tanner, Elizabeth Elam x Tanner. S/ John Tucker, Blanch x Tucker. *(See DB 5-112above.) (See also DB 18-125 below.)*

DB 17-378, 7 Jan 1786, rec. 22 Jun 1786, John Tucker & wf Blanch of Warren Co., N. C., to Lodowick Talley of Amelia Co., for L400., 200 ac. bo. John Olds's cor., Thomas Booth's line, Dyson's cor. & line. Wit: Field Tanner, Robert Tanner, Daniel Talley. S/ John x Tucker.

*(No deed was found for the purchase of his land by John Tucker. However see Patent 22-522 above.)*

*(Lodowick Talley was uncle of subject John Tucker Jr.)*

DB 18-125, 28 Jun 1787. John Tucker & wf Blanch of Warren Co., N.C., for 5 Sh. to dau. Blanch Tanner, one negro wench named Sue with her increase. Wit: Jeremiah Tanner, Wm. Clardy, Daniel Wilkerson. S/ John Tucker, Blanch x Tucker.

*NOTE: It appears that John Tucker & wf Blanch had a dau Blanch Tucker who md a Tanner, possibly Edward Tanner. See DB 6-433 above.*

DB 20-133, 16 Mar 1795, rec. 22 Oct 1795, John Tucker (jr?) of Warren Co., N. C. to Rice Newman of Amelia Co., for L5., 80 ac. on Wintocomake Cr. adj. John Tabb & Rice Newman. Wit: James Worsham, John Worsham, George Bevill. S/ John Tucker. *(No deed was found for the purchase of this land by John Tucker.)*

## LIST OF TITHES

| 1753 | 2 | John Tucker, Lucy. |
|------|-------|----------------------------------------------|
| 1755 | 2 | John Tucker, Lucy. |
| 1756 | 2 | John Tucker Jr, Lucy. |
| 1762 | 2 | John Tucker, will, Lucy. |
| 1763 | 2 - 300 | John Tucker, Lucy. |
| 1765 | 2 - 200 | John Tucker (Waller's son), Lucy. |
| 1767 | 2 - 200 | John Tucker (Waller), Lucy. |
| 1768 | 2 - 200 | John Tucker (Waller), Lucy. |
| 1769 | 3 - 200 | John Tucker (Waller), John Tucker, Lucy. |
| 1770 | 2 - 200 | John Tucker, Lucy. |

## LAND TAX RECORDS

| 1782 | John Tucker Jr | 200 ac. |
|------|----------------|---------|
| 1787 | John Tucker Jr | 200 ac. |

## SUMMARY:

John Tucker Jr's mother Ann died ca 1726 and his father John Sr died in 1727, and he was most probably raised by his grandparents John & Anna Talley.

John Tucker Jr was age 1.5 when his grandfather John Tally wrote his will in 1726, and age 16 when his grandfather died in 1740. His mother Ann must have died prior to 1726, for she was not named in the will of her father John Tally, but he did will 100 ac. land to his grandson John Tucker (Jr) in 1740.

At age 16, following his grandfather's death in 1740, John Tucker Jr selected John Waller as his guardian, from whom he bought 200 ac. upon reaching age 21 in 1745.

John Tucker Jr, son of John Tucker Sr. & wife Ann Tally, b 1722 in Pr. George Co., moved to Warren Co. NC ca 1786, md Blanch before 1746, & had issue:

Blanch Tucker, md c1787? Edward Tanner.

1. Boddie, John B., "Births 1720-1792 from the Bristol Parish Register of Henrico, Prince George and Dinwiddie."

2. Weisiger, Benjamin B. III, "Prince George County, Virginia Wills & Deeds 1713-1728", 1973

3. Card File of Land Patents and Grants, Virginia State Library Archives

# T0122000 - FRANCIS TUCKER

## MD SARAH ____

### SON OF JOHN TUCKER SR

### MD ANN TALLY

BRISTOL PARISH REGISTER [1]

francis Son of John and Ann tucker born 3d Janr 1726.

DB 1-531, 17 Jul 1741, Bond. Francis Tucker, orphan of John Tucker, has chosen William Traylor as his guardian. Sec. John Waller. L100. (ca age 15)

The subject Francis Tucker became age 21 in 1747, but no other record was found for him in Amelia Co.

He may be the Francis Tucker who bought and patented land in Halifax Co. Va.

HALIFAX CO. VA.

DB 3-341, 20 May 1762, rec 20 May 1762, William Byrd of Charles City Co., Va. to Francis Tucker of Halifax Co., Va., for 20 shillings, 90 ac. on Hyco Ri. S/ W Byrd by David Caldwell, his power of attorney. *(See DB 8-459.)*

DB 7-122, 5 Sep 1767, rec 9 May 1768, John Swelervant (or Sullivant) to Francis Tucker, for L40, 150 ac. on Hico Cr., bo Nash Glidwell, Nashs Br. S/ John Swelervant. Wit: Sith x Pettypool, George Boyd, William x Pettypool, Peter Overby.

DB 8-459, 19 Jul 1772, rec 15 Oct 1772, Francis Tucker to David Christopher, for L50, 90 ac., on Hico Ri.,,, bo. Nash Glidwell. S/ Francis x Tucker, Sarah x Tucker. Wit: Stephen Watson, John Williams, Nash x Glidwell. *(See DB 3-341.)*

> *NOTE: The signature of Sarah Tucker indicates she was wife of Francis Tucker.*

DB 9-304 List of surveys by surveyor of Halifax Co. since commencement of year 1771. included 24 Oct 1771, Francis Tucker 384 ac. on draughts of Blue Wing (Cr); and 6 May 1773 Francis Tucker 332 ac. draughts of Morrises & Aarons Cr. Rec. 14 Jun 1774.

WB 1-246, 16 Nov 1777, wp 19 Nov 1778, will of Henry Tally, names: sons Henry & John Tally; Susannah, Mary & Abraham Tally; Littlepage, Anderson & Sally Tally. Exors:: Any two of Abraham Tally, Francis Tucker, Henry Tally, & John Tally. Wit: Obadiah Overbey, Jesse Rakestraw, John Tucker.

PATENT C-251, Francis Tucker, Feb 1, 1781. Halifax Co. Va. 184 ac. on draughts of Bluewing, beg. at Moores Cor., in the Country line, adj. Richard Anrews & c.

The Land Tax Records of Halifax Co., Va. show Sarah Tucker holding 400 ac. beginning 1787-1794 in the Southern District.

*NOTE: Little Blue Wing Cr. empties into Blue Wing Cr., which empties into Hyco Ri., which empties into the southside of the Banister Ri, all of which are in the Southern District of Halifax Co., Va.*

1. Boddie, John B., "Births 1720-1792 from the Bristol Parish Register of Henrico, Prince George and Dinwiddie."

# T0130000 - HENRY TUCKER

## MD 1ST ELIZABETH _____,
## MD 2ND AMY _____

## SON OF FRANCIS TUCKER
## THE ELDER

## MD MARY _____

PRINCE GEORGE CO. VA.

Will, p663, Will of Francis Tucker of Bristol Parish, d 12 Dec 1722, p 10 Dec 1723.

Son, Francis, land on n.e. side of Mawhipponoak Cr. lower end.

son John, land n.s. same creek, joining Henry Mayes.

son Henry, land bet. sons Francis & John, inc. plantation where I now live.

son Abram, land n.s. Mawhipponoak Cr. joining son Henry & Thomas Mitchell.

son Mathew, land joining Thomas Mitchell.

All goods to be equally divided bet. children & wife Mary.

Wit: Mathew Mayes, Henry Mayes, John Powell. S/ Francis x Tucker.

> *NOTE: The lands which Francis Tucker the Elder willed to his sons lay in the area which was separated from Prince George Co. in 1752 to form Dinwiddie Co, and only fragmented records remain for either county.*

> *NOTE: The subject Henry Tucker was born prior to 1722, when he was named in the will of his father Francis Tucker (the Elder) who married Mary. He was probably b c1707, and may be father to the children named below:*

BRISTOL PARISH REGISTER [1]

Elizabeth D of Henry & _____ Tucker Born 2d Sepr 1729.

_____ D of Henry & Elizabeth Tucker Born 8th May 1731 Bapt 29th august.

Frances of Henry & amy Tucker Born 25th apr 1733 Bapt June 3d.

*NOTE: Henry Tucker son of Francis Tucker the Elder & wife Mary, had a nephew Henry Tucker b ca 1742 son of Matthew Tucker Sr. of Amelia Co.*

*Nothing more is known of the subject Henry Tucker family.*

SUMMARY:

Henry Tucker, son of Francis Tucker the Elder & wf Mary, b c1707, probably in Prince George Co., may have md 1st ca 1728 Elizabeth ___, and may have md 2nd ca 1732 Amy ___, and had issue:

Elizabeth Tucker b 1729 of Elizabeth.

(a daughter) b 1731 of Elizabeth.

Frances Tucker b 1733 of Amy.

1. Boddie, John B., "Births 1720-1792 from the Bristol Parish Register of Henrico, Prince George and Dinwiddie."

# T0140000 - ABRAM TUCKER

## MD HELENOUR ____

## SON OF FRANCIS TUCKER
## THE ELDER

## MD MARY ____

PRINCE GEORGE CO. VA.

Will, p663, Will of Francis Tucker of Bristol Parish, d 12 Dec 1722, p 10 Dec 1723.

Son, Francis, land on n.e. side of Mawhipponoak Cr. lower end.

son John, land n.s. same creek, joining Henry Mayes.

son Henry, land bet. sons Francis & John, inc. plantation where I now live.

son Abram, land n.s. Mawhipponoak Cr. joining son Henry & Thomas Mitchell.

son Mathew, land joining Thomas Mitchell.

All goods to be equally divided bet. children & wife Mary.

Wit: Mathew Mayes, Henry Mayes, John Powell. S/ Francis x Tucker.

*NOTE: The lands which Francis Tucker the Elder willed to his sons lay in the area which was separated from Prince George Co. in 1752 to form Dinwiddie Co, and only fragmented records remain for either county.*

*NOTE: The subject Abram Tucker was born prior to 1722 when he was named in the will of his father Francis Tucker (the Elder) who married Mary. He was probably born prior to 1719, and probably was the father named below:*

BRISTOL PARISH REGISTER [1]

Miles. S. of Abram & Helenour Tuckers Born Feby 16th 1741-2 & Bapt Mar. 14th 1741-42.

*NOTE: The subject Abram Tucker also may be the same as Abraham Tucker who patented land in 1751, and may have had a son or grandson Abraham Tucker who patented land in 1808.*

PATENTS [2]

Patent 31-49, 20 Sep 1751, Abraham Tucker, Prince George Co., 100 ac. s.s. Blackwater Swamp, adj. Thomas Williams.

Patent 56-495, 8 Nov 1808, Abraham Tucker, Prince George Co., 23 ac. adj. Abraham, Ally, Edwards.

SUMMARY:

Abram Tucker, son of Francis Tucker the Elder & wf Mary, b probably ca 1719 in Prince George Co., probably md ca 1740 Heleanor _?_, and had issue:

Miles Tucker b 1741-42.

1. Broddie, John B., "Births 1720-1792 from the Bristol Parish Register of Henrico, Prince George and Dinwiddie."

2. Card File, Land Patents and Grants, Virginia State Library Archives

# T0150000 - MATTHEW TUCKER (SR) (I)

## SON OF FRANCIS TUCKER
## THE ELDER

### MD MARY ____

PRINCE GEORGE CO. VA. [1]

p 663, Will of Francis Tucker of Bristol Parish, d 12 Dec 1722, p 10 Dec 1723.

Son, Francis, land on n.e. side of Mawhipponoak Cr. lower end.
son John, land n.s. same creek, joining Henry Mayes.
son Henry, land bet. sons Francis & John, inc. plantation where I now live.
son Abram, land n.s. Mawhipponoak Cr. joining son Henry & Thomas Mitchell.
son Mathew, land joining Thomas Mitchell.
All goods to be equally divided bet. children & wife Mary.
Wit: Mathew Mayes, Henry Mayes, John Powell. S/ Francis x Tucker.

p 756, Survey, 10 Feb 1720. Matthew Tucker, son of Francis Tucker on w.s. of Mawhipponoak Cr.. 99 ac. *(See Patent 14-308.)*

*NOTE: Matthew Tucker must have been at least age 21 when he surveyed land in 1720, so he must have been born as early as 1699.*

PATENT [2]

Patent 14-308, 25 Aug 1731, Matthew Tucker, Pr. Geo. Co., 99 ac. u.s. or w.s. of Mawhipponock Cr. *(See Survey 1720.)*

DINWIDDIE CO. VA.

1752 Dinwiddie Co. was formed from Prince George Co.

*NOTE: The lands which Matthew Tucker received by the will of his father Francis Tucker the Elder, and the land which he surveyed and patented on Mawhipponock Cr. lay in the area which became Dinwiddie Co. Only fragmented records remain for either Prince George or Dinwiddie county.*

# AMELIA CO. VA.

1735 Amelia Co. was formed from that part of Prince George Co. which lay north and west (upper side) of Namozine Cr.

## LIST OF TITHABLES

| 1740 | 1 | Matthew Tucker |
|------|---|----------------|
| 1741 | 1 | Matthew Tucker |
| 1744 | 1 | Matthew Tucker |
| 1747 | 1 | Matthew Tucker |
| 1750 | 1 | Matthew Tucker |
| 1751 | 1 | Matthew Tucker |
| 1752 | 2 | Matthew Tucker, Matthew Tucker Jun |
| 1753 | 2 | Matthew Tucker, Matthew Tucker Jun |
| 1755 | 3 | Matthew Tucker, Matthew Tucker Jun, Thomas Tucker |
| 1756 | 3 | Matthew Tucker, Matthew Tucker Jun, Thomas Tucker |
| 1762 | 2 | Matthew Tucker, Henry Tucker |
| 1763 | 1-100 | Matthew Tucker Sen |
| 1765 | 1-100 | Matthew Tucker Sen |
| 1767 | 1-100 | Matthew Tucker Sen |
| 1769 | 1-100 | Matthew Tucker Sen |
| 1770 | 1-100 | Matthew Tucker Sen |
| 1782 | 2 | Matthew Tucker Sr (levy free), Sam Anthony |

*(See WB 3-291, 1785, Matthew Tucker).*

## LAND TAX RECORDS

1782 Matthew Tucker 100 ac.

*NOTE: No births of children of Mathew Tucker are recorded in the Bristol Parish Register. But from the listing of 16-yr-up tithable sons in the Tithable Records, it is estimated that Matthew Tucker Jr was b ca 1736, Thomas Tucker b ca 1739, Henry Tucker b ca 1742.*

DB 1-149, 11 Aug 1738, John x Parish to William Parish for L14.10., 150 ac. on s.s. Wintocomake Cr., below main & upper fk., bo. by Great Branch & line of Matthew Tucker.

DB 1-257, 20 Aug 1740, William Parish to Henry Talley for L26.,

150 ac. s.s. Wintocomake Cr. below main upper fk., bound in pt. by Matthew Tucker's line on the Great Branch & a cr. Rec. 20 Aug 1740. Amey, wf. of Wm. Parrish ack. dower int.

*NOTE: The above 2 deeds, referring to land bounding Matthew Tucker, indicate that Matthew Tucker owned land in Amelia Co. prior to Aug 1740. This land was probably acquired prior to 1735, while Amelia Co. was still a part of Pr. Geo. Co., (for which only fragmented records are available), and was most probably the land whereon Matthew Tucker lived and willed to sons Thomas and Henry. (See WB 3-291.)*

Patent 21-120, Matthew Tucker, 20‾ Jul 1742, Amelia Co., 400 ac. l.s. Wintercomaick Cr. adj. William Tisdale & c. *(See DB 3-59 for 190 ac. & DB 3-62 for 210 ac..)*

DB 3-59, 10 Dec 1747, Matthew Tucker to Parmenas Palmer, for L12., 190 ac. bo. Fran. Tucker's line, Henry Talley's line, William Tisdale's line. Wit: Richard (R) Talley, William (H) Hood, John (I) Tucker. *(See Patent 21-120.)*

DB 3-61, 18 May 1748, Fran. Tucker To Matthew Tucker for L7, 100 ac, bo Thomas Hood, Fran. Tucker, Peter Coleman, Godfrey Coleman, Crawley. Wit: Parmonas Palmer, William Palmer, William (H) Hood.

DB 3-62, 25 Jan 1747, Matthew Tucker to William Hood for L7.10., 210 ac. bo. Parmonas Palmer's new line, William Tisdale's line, John Hood's line, Thomas Hood's line, Fran. Tucker's line. Wit: Parmonas Palmer, William Palmer, Fran (C) Tucker. *(See Patent 21-210.)*

WB 3-291, will of Matthew Tucker Sr, wd 3 Mar 1784, *(wp not shown -See WB 3-357)*, names:
dau. Phoebe Tucker - negro Isbell, 5 head cattle, bed & furn., for life, then to son Matthew Tucker.
son Thomas Tucker - plantation whereon I now live.
son Henry Tucker - the part of land now in his possession.
Ex: son Matthew Tucker, and Absolom Tucker.
Wit: Absolom Tucker, Joseph Bevill (?), Paschal Tucker.

S/ Matthew Tucker.

WB 3-357, Est. I&A, Matthew Tucker, decd, 20 Jun 1785, by Evans Mitchell, Joseph Bevill, John Morgan.

*NOTE: It is assumed Matthew Tucker Sr. died in 1785.*

NOTTOWAY CO. VA.

1789 Nottoway Co. was formed from Amelia Co

WB 2-328, will of Phebe Tucker, wd 22 Aug 1800, wp 1 Jan 1807. Nottoway Co.
Leg: brother Matthew Tucker - negro woman Isabelle & her increase. Milly Branch Clardy - dovetail chest.
Ex: Jordan Cranshaw & Thomas Echols. Wit: Alain Cranshaw, Judith Cranshaw. S/ Phebe x Tucker.

WB 3-338, 20 Jan 1807. I&A Est Phebe Tucker. Included slaves Isabella, Jack, Ross, Tom, Lyda, Mary, Stephen, Peter, Hot, Amy, Laming, Ellecks.

SUMMARY:

Matthew Tucker Sr (I), son of Francis Tucker the Elder & wf Mary, b ca 1699 probably in Charles City Co., d 1785 in Amelia Co. His wife probably preceded him in death, and was not named in his deeds or will. They had issue:

Matthew Tucker Jr (II) b ca 1736

Thomas Tucker b ca 1739, or earlier.

Henry Tucker b ca 1742.

Phebe Tucker b ____, d 1807 Nottoway Co.

1. Weisiger, Benjamin B. III, "Prince George County, Virginia Wills & Deeds 1713-1728", 1973
2. Card File of Land Patents and Grants, Virginia State Library Archives

# T0151000 - MATTHEW TUCKER JR (II)

## MD 1ST RACHAEL ____,
## MD 2ND ELIZABETH REASE

### SON OF MATTHEW TUCKER SR (I)

AMELIA CO. VA.

WB 3-291, will of Matthew Tucker Sr., wd 3 Mar 1784, *(wp not shown -See W83-357.),*
names:
dau. Phoebe Tucker - negro Isbell, 5 head cattle, bed & furn., for life, then to son Matthew Tucker.
son Thomas Tucker - plantation whereon I now live.
son Henry Tucker - the part of land now in his possession.
Ex: son Matthew Tucker, and Absolom Tucker.
Wit: Absolom Tucker, Joseph Bevill (?), Paschal Tucker.
S/ Matthew Tucker.

WB 3-357, Est. I&A, Matthew Tucker, decd, 20 Jun 1785, by Evans Mitchell, Joseph Bevill, John Morgan.

*NOTE: It is assumed Matthew Tucker Sr (I) died in 1785.*

DB 6-50, 26 Mar 1757, John Smith & wf Martha to Matthew Tucker Junr, for L6.9, 75 ac., bo. Tucker's Br., Peter Coleman's line, Matthew Tucker Junr's corner. Thomas Hood's line. Wit: Matt'w Wills, Ben Bowles, John Hood.

DB 7-695, 27 Oct 1762, William Hood Junr to Matthew Tucker Junr., for L25., 100 ac. bo. mouth of Bull Br., Horsepen Br., Abraham Hood's line, Francis Tucker's line, Matthew Tucker's line, Tucker's Br. Wit: John Hood, Michael Clandy, Edward Tanner. Rec.28 Oct 1762. S/ William x Hood.

DB 8-22, 24 Nov 1762, Matthew Tucker Junr & wf Rachael, to Thomas Beary of King William Co., for L23., 75 ac. bo. Tucker's Br., on Thomas Hood's line, Peter Coleman's line, Matthew Tucker Senr's cor. Rec 25 Nov 1762. S/ Matthew Tucker.

DB 9-47. 24 Sep 1766, Francis Tucker Sen & wf Ann to Matthew Tucker Jun, for Le, 16 ac. on Horsepen Br. on Abram Hood's line, sd Matthew

Tucker's Spring Br. & line. Wit: Henry (x) Tucker, Thomas (x) Tucker, Wm. Hall. Rec. 25 Sep 1766. S/ Francis (x) Tucker, Ann (x) Tucker.

DB 13-156, 10 Apr 1775, John Hughes to Matthew Tucker Jun., for L45., 200 ac., bo. dividing line btwn. Eckles & Hightower. Rec. 27 Apr 1775. Wife Ann relinq. dower.

DB 17-27, 29 Oct 1783, William Brannon of 96 District, state of N.C. to Matthew Tucker Jr. of Amelia Co., fir L50., 100 ac. bo. Bottom's cor. & line. Wit: Edmund Wills, Joseph Bevill Jr., Elizabeth Wills. S/ William Brannon

DB 17-93. 30 Sep 1784, Samuel Morgan to Matthew Tucker, for L200., 130 ac., bo. by lands of Thomas Bottom, Francis Wallace, Richard Livesay, Richard Locke decd., Thomas Eckles, & joining 100 ac. of sd Tucker known by the name of Leonard's Old Field. Wit: Ben Alfiend(?), William Sydnor, _____ . S./ Mary x Morgan. *(See DB 17-27.)*

DB 17-95, 5 Oct 1784, Matthew Tucker Jun & wf Rachael, to John Morgan, for L100., 116 ac., bo. Matthew Tucker's spring br., Matthew Tucker Sr's line, Evan Mitchell's line, Bull Br., Abraham Hood's line, Horsepen Br. Wit: Richard Walthall, Paschal Tucker. Rec. 28 Oct 1785. S/ Matthew x Tucker, Rachael Tucker.

LIST OF TITHABLES

1762  1-100 Matthew Tucker Jr
1765  1-116 Matthew Tucker Jr
1769  2-116 Matthew Tucker Jr, Jack
1770  2-116 Matthew Tucker Jr, Jack
1781  4      Matthew Tucker, Pascall Tucker, Jack, Sam

PERSONAL TAX RECORDS

1782  3      Matthew Tucker, Jack, Bob
1783  3      Matthew Tucker
1784  5      Matthew Tucker
1785  3      Matthew Tucker
1786  2      Matthew Tucker

## PERSONAL TAX RECORDS

1787  2    Matthew Tucker, Parskill Tucker

1788  1    Matthew Tucker

## LAND TAX RECORDS

1782  Matthew Tucker Jr, 116 ac. Raleigh Parish

1782  Matthew Tucker 200 ac. Nottoway Parish
1784  alterations - Matthew Tucker Jr by John Morgan 116
1787  alterations – Matthew Tucker Jr by Henry Tucker 50, by
Thomas Tucker 50

> *NOTE: The above alterations are confusing. See DB 17-95 for 116 ac. Matthew Tucker Jr to John Morgan. As to the 1787 alteration: Matthew Tucker Sr. owned 100 ac. at time of his will, and gave to son Thomas - plantation whereon I live, and to son Henry -land in his possession. The intent of the alteration is probably that Matthew Jr as executor, passed 50 ac. to Thomas and 50 ac. to Henry.*

## MARRIAGES - AMELIA CO.

13 Nov 1786 Isham Eckles and Philadelphia Tucker, dau of Matt. Tucker (II). Sur. Matt. Tucker. *(Note: Isham Eckles was son of Thomas Eckles.)*

22 Dec 1787, Paschal Tucker to Tabitha Eckles. Sec. Edward Eckles, Parent Thomas Eckles. *(Note: Paschal Tucker was son of Matthew Tucker II.)*

22 Dec 1787 Edward Eckles and Belsiaucker, dau of Matthew Tucker (II) who consents. Sur. Paschal Tucker. *(Note: Edward Eckles was son of Thomas Eckles.)*

17 Mar 1788, Mathew Tucker to Elizabeth Rease. Sec. Js. Holmes. *(Note: This must be the second marriage of Matthew Tucker II.)*

## NOTTOWAY CO. VA.

1789 Nottoway Co. formed from Amelia Co.

> *NOTE: Following the death of his father Matthew Tucker*

*Sr (I), Matthew Tucker Jr (II) now calls himself Matthew Tucker Sr, and himself has a son Matthew Tucker Jr. (III).*

## LAND TAX RECORDS

| 1789-91 | Matthew Tucker    | $200 + 230 = 430$ ac.                 |
|---------|-------------------|---------------------------------------|
| 1792-98 | Matthew Tucker    | 430 ac.                               |
| 1802-03 | Matthew Tucker Sr | $430 + 242 = 672$ ac.                 |
| 1804-13 | Matthew Tucker Sr | $430 + 142 = 572$ ac. on Hurricane Cr |

DB 2-291, 1 Apr 1800, rec 1 Apr 1802, Bottoms Steagall of Brunswick Co. to Matthew Tucker of Nottoway Co., 243.5 ac. on waters of Hurricane Swamp, bo. Wallis, Beacher, Spain, Anderson, Tucker. S/ Bottom Steagall.

DB 2-436, 31 Aug 1803, Matthew Tucker to Paschal Tucker, both of Nottoway Co., for love & good will, gift of 100 ac., on Hurricane Swamp, bo. Cates, Leonard, Hightower, Cryer. S/ Matthew x Tucker Wit: Saunders Crenshaw, James Eckles, Truman Eckles.

DB 3-222, 10 Dec 1798, rec 1 Jan 1807, Charles Anderson & wf Nancy, to Matthew Tucker Junr, for L9., 20 ac.., bo. Steagal, Griggs. S/ Charles Anderson, Nancy Anderson. Wit: Herbert Tucker, Thos. Eckles.

*NOTE: The above deed says Matthew Tucker Jr. Following the death of his father, Matthew Tucker Jr became Matthew Tucker Sr, who in WB 4-63 below, gave land bought of Charles Anderson to son Matthew Tucker.*

WB 2-163, wd 6 Mar 1805, wp 6 Jun 1805, will of Paschal Tucker of Nottoway Co. Va. named:
wife Tabitha - all real & personal estate for life.
nephew Joel Tucker (son of my brother Matthew Tucker) all my land, plus 2/3 of increase of two female negroes Mary & Annaca.
Niece Sally Eckles (dau. of Edwd Eckles) -- 1/3 of increase of negroes Mary & Annaca.
At death of wife, balance of estate to Nephew Joel Tucker & Niece Sally Eckles.
Exor: wife Tabitha & friend Freeman Eckles. S/ Paschal Tucker. Wit: Ephraim Eckles, Joel Eckles, James Eckles.

WB 2-281, 5 Jun 1806, Inv. of Est of Paschal Tucker, included one negro woman Mary, 3 heads horses, 1 Sorrell, 1 Bay, 7 cows, 27 hogs, furniture, & household items. S/ Tabitha x Tucker, Samuel Echols.

WB 2-328, wd 22 Aug 1806, wp ____ Jul 1807, will of Phebe Tucker of Nottoway Co., names:
Bro. Matthew Tucker, negro woman named Isabell & all her increase.
Milly Branch Clardy - dovetail chest.
Exor: ____ Crenshaw & Thomas Eckols. S/ Phebe x Tucker.
Wit: Alain Crenshaw, Judith Crenshaw.

WB 2-338, 26 Jan 1807, Inv. & Appr. of Est of Phebe Tucker, included 12 slaves Isabell, Jack, Rafe, Tom, Lyda, Mary, Stephen, Peter, Hal, Amy, Sam, Ellerby, & 1 pine chest.

WB 4-63, wd 11 Jan 1810, wp 5 Jun 1817. will of Matthew Tucker Senr. of Nottoway Co.,
Son Matthew Tucker - the land whereon he now lives & bo. by land of Bottom Stegall & including all the land I bought of Charles Anderson, but no part of the land I bought of Bottom Stegall.
Son Lewellen Tucker - L44. in addition to what I have already advanced for him.
Wife, (not named) for life or widowhood, best male slaves I have, best horse, best feather bed, furniture & priviledge of living where I now live & making a reasonable use of my plantation to support her & her property.
Dau. Dicey - one feather bed & furniture as good as those given to my other daughters. (not named)
Son Harbert - all rest of my land subject to provision made for my wife. I relinquish all claim to negro woman Milley which my wife brought with her.
Balance of estate to be equally divided btwn all my children, and three daughters of my daughter Susanah Clardy be considered as one of my children & entitled to one share to be equally divided btwn them when they marry or come of lawful age.
Exors: friends Saml Morgan, Richard Epes, Saunders Crenshaw & my son Harbert Tucker. S/ Matthew x Tucker Senr. Wit: Saml G. Williams, Thomas Morgan, Thomas Fitzgerald.

CODICIL, 26 Jul 1816, Whereas son Harbert Tucker has died & left widow & five chlldren, I give to those five children all that part of my estate which I had given to their father, equally divided btwn them, reserving enjoyment of same to my son's widow for life or widowhood. S/ Matthew x Tucker.
Wit: William Crenshaw, Joseph W. Crenshaw, Sand Morgan.

5 Jun 1817, Last Will & Testament of Matthew Tucker Senr cecd with Codicil exhibited into court by Samuel Morgan, and same contested by Edward Eckles, & continued to next court.

7 Aug 1817, same was again offered for proof & contested as aforesaid. After testimony, will and codicil ordered to be recorded. Samuel Morgan & Richard Epes refused to take upon themselves the burden of Executors.

Order Book 8-48, 2 Oct 1817, Elizabeth Tucker is appointed special Guardian to the orphans of Harbert Tucker decd.
*(Note: it is assumed Elizabeth is the widow of Harbert and the mother of his orphans.)*

Order Book 8-48, 2 Oct 1817, Elizabeth Tucker widow and relict of Matthew Tucker Senr decd -vs- Matthew Tucker & Elizabeth Tucker, and Patsey E. Tucker, Spencer G. Tucker, Elizabeth A. Tucker, Matthew J. Tucker and Joshua G. Tucker, infants of tender years by Elizabeth Tucker their Guardian - - ordered that Samuel Morgan, Samuel B. Jeter, Bartelot P. Todd, Joel Eckles and or any three of them, attended by a competent surveyor, do lay off, allot & assign to complainant, one third part of land of Matthew Tucker Senr late, to hold as her dower.

Order Book 8-50, 2 Oct 1817, Matthew Tucker Senr having been dead three months, and no person having applied for adm. of his estate, It is ordered that Samuel Morgan Sheriff of this County, administer the estate according to law.

Order Book 8-51, 2 Oct 1817, Elizabeth Tucker widow & relict of Matthew Tucker Snr decd, -vs- Samuel Morgan Sheriff -- ordered to divide personal estate of Matthew Tucker Senr decd & allot & assign to complainant one third part as her dower.

Order Book 8-84, 4 Dec 1817, Matthew Tucker, Isham Eckles & wf Delphia, Edward Eckles & wf Elizabeth, Abraham Stow & wf Letty, Lewelling Tucker, Nancy Bovill, Elizabeth Tucker, Carter Hudgings & wf Rachel, Dicey Tucker, Polly Clardy, Milly Clardy and Burwell Hudgins and wf Elizabeth -vs- Samuel Morgan Sheriff - - decreed & ordered to divide estate of Matthew Tucker Senr decd according to residuary clause in his will disposing of balance of his estate.

WB 4-89, 13 Dec 1817, Inv & appr of est of Matthew Tucker Senr, by B.P. Todd for Saml Morgan & admr. Alan Cranshaw, Wm. Crenshaw, James Williams. Included negro men Jack, Ralph, Bob, negro boys Hale, Sam, Patrick, Ellick, Potram, negro woman Isbel, negro woman Mary & child Peter, negro woman Lizzie, negro woman Amey, negro woman Milly & child Albert, negro girls Annica, Hannah, & negro boys Ned, Peter.

WB 4-90, 16th & 17th Dec 1817, rec. 1 Jan 1818. Acct of Sales of est. of Matthew Tucker Senr, by Bartlett P. Todd, DS for Saml Morgan. Names included Tabitha Moon, Edward Eckles, Braxton P. Eckles, William Leonard, Wiley Eckles, Matthew Tucker, Carter Hudgins, Thomas Eckles, Joseph Sheffield, Ling(?) Tucker. Mrs. Elizabeth Tucker Sr., Elizabeth Tucker Jr., Kennon Spain, Isham Eckles, John G. W. Holloway, Benjamin Booth, Thomas Hudgins, Frances L. Mosely, Benjamin Clardy, James Williams, Spencer Spain, William Buttes(?), Griffin Gunn, Peter Clark, John B. Holmes, Anderson Vaughan, Charles A. Livesey, Samuel G. Williams, Samuel Morgan, Joel Tucker, Dicey Tucker, William T. Wells, John B. Clark, Thomas Moon, David Bridgforth.

Order Book 8-261, 6 Mar 1819, Elizabeth Tucker, widow & relict of Matthew Tucker Sr., -vs- Matthew Tucker and Elizabeth Tucker, and Patsey E. Tucker, Spencer G. Tucker, Elizabeth A. Tucker, Matthew J. Tucker, and Joshua G. Tucker infants - - commissioners layed off and assigned to Mrs., Elizabeth Tucker, widow of Matthew Tucker, Senr decd, one third of the land, 197 ac., as dower for life.

*NOTE: If 197 ac. represents one third of land of Matthew Tucker decd, then he owned approximately 591 ac. at time of his death.*

Order Book 8-262, 6 Mar 1819, Elizabeth Tucker widow & relict of Matthew Tucker Senr decd -vs- Samuel Morgan Sheriff - commissioners assigned to Elizabeth Tucker, 7 slaves: Albert, Anica, Ned, Nanner, Peter & Jack, ___ , being her dower.

Order Book 8-265, 6 Mar 1819, Matthew Tucker, Isham Eckles & wf Delphia, Edward Eckles & wf Elizabeth, Abraham Stow & wf Letty, Lewelling Tucker, Nancy Bevill, Elizabeth Tucker, Carter Hudgings & wf Rachel, Dicey Tucker, Polly Clardy, Milly Clardy & Burwell Hudgings & wf Elizabeth -vs- Bartlett P. Todd deputy Sheriff – commissioners divided into 10 parts, the property slaves of Matthew Tucker decd: Bob, Isabel, Patram, Ralph, Eliza, Mary & her son Peter, Hall, Sam, Ellick, Amy & Patrick, & assigned 1/10th part each to Nancy Beville, Mrs. Susanna Clardy's heirs, Edward Eckles & wf Elizabeth, Matthew Tucker Jr, Lewelling Tucker, Mrs. Elizabeth Tucker widow of Herbert Tucker decd, Dicy N Tucker, Isham Eckles & wf Delphia, Abraham Stow & wf Letty, Carter Hudgings & wf Rachel.

*NOTE: Although the subject Matthew Tucker Sr (II) did not name his deceased son Paschal in his will, the above order seems to identify his 10 other children, namely: Nancy, Susanna, Elizabeth, Matthew Jr, Lewelling, Herbert, Dicy, Delphia, Letty & Rachel.*

*NOTE: Paschal Tucker who died 1805, was first listed as a 16-yr-up tithable in the household of his father in Amelia Co. in 1781, so he was born ca 1765, the son of Matthew Tucker Sr (II) & 1st wife Rachael.*

*NOTE: The will of Paschal Tucker (Nottoway Co. WB 2-163 probated 6 Jun 1805), identifies a "nephew Joel Tucker, as son of my brother Matthew Tucker". It appears then that Paschal Tucker was a half-brother of Matthew Tucker (III), and son of Matthew Tucker (II), (1736-1817), and grandson of Matthew Tucker (I), (1699-1785).*

WB 4-223, rec 6 Jul 1820. Est. of Matthew Tucker Senr. in acct. with Samuel Morgan Sherrif & Adm. Cash paid to Lewellin Tucker.

SUMMARY OF LAND TRANSACTIONS:

| | | | PLUS | MINUS | BAL |
|---|---|---|---|---|---|
| 1757 DB 6-50 | fr Smith | | 75 (1) | | 75 |
| 1762 DB 7-695 | fr Hood | | 100 (2) | | 175 |
| 1762 DB 8-22 | to Beary | | | 75 (1) | 100 |
| 1765 DB 9-47 | fr gf Fran. Tucker Sr | 16 (2) | | | 116 |
| 1775 DB 13-156 | fr Hughes | | 100 | | 316 |
| 1783 DB 17-27 | fr Brannon | | 100 | | 416 |
| 1784 DB 17-93 | fr S. Morgan | | 130 | | 546 |
| 1784 DB 17-95 | to J. Morgan | | | 116 (2) | 430 |
| 1800 DB 2-291 | fr Steagall | | 243.5 | | 673.5 |
| 1803 DB 2-436 | to son Paschal | | | 100 | 573.5 |
| 1807 DB 3-222 | fr Anderson | | 20 | | 593.5 |
| 1817 WB 4-63 | to Wf Elizabeth- dower | | | 197 | 376.5 |
| | to son Matthew | | | | |
| | to son Harbert | | | | |

*NOTE: The wife of Matthew Tucker Jr-Sr (II) is identified as Rachael in DB 8-22 in 1762 and DB 17-95 in 1784. Matthew did not identify his wife by name in Nottoway WB 4-63, dated 1810, prorated 1817. But Nottoway Co. records indicate his widow was Elizabeth. Matthew Tucker m (2nd wf) Elizabeth Reese in 1788, so (1st wf) Rachael must have died prior to 1788. The parents of Elizabeth wife of Matthew II is not determined. The wife of Harbert Tucker (son of Matthew II) was also named Elizabeth, and she is believed to be dau of James Eckles Sr. The widow of Matthew Sr (II) was known as "Elizabeth Sr"; the widow of Harbert was known as "Elizabeth Jr". There were several marriages in Amelia Co between the Tucker and Eckles families.*

WB 3-___ , wd 8 Oct 1815, wp 6 Jun 1816, will of James Eckles Sr., names sons James, Ephriam, Joel, Freeman; daughters Patsey

Eckles, Bethiah River, Priscilla Hightower, Elizabeth Tucker. Wit: William River, Thomas Eckles, Sam'l Morgan.

Order Book 8-477, Nov 1816, further identifies legatees of James Eckles Sr. as: James Eckles Jr; Ephriam Eckles; Joel Eckles; Freeman Eckles & his children Allen, Gibson, Martha, Polly B. & Frances; Patsey Eckles; Robert Rivers & wf Bethia, formerly Bethia Eckles; Joshua Hightower & wf Priscilla, formerly Priscilla Eckles; Elizabeth Tucker, formerly Elizabeth Eckles; and Thomas Eckles & his children James A, Wm, & Clement Eckles.

Order Book 5-167, 5 Jul 1807 identifies legatees of Thomas Eckles as: Isham Eckles executor; Joel Eckles; Charnel Hightower & wf Sall, formerly Salley Eckles; George Turner & wf Elizabeth, formerly Elizabeth Eckles; Edward Eckles; Francis Eckles; Thomas Eckles; Tabitha Tucker, formerly Tabitha Eckles: Joel Eckles & wf Polly, formerly Polly Eckles; Matthew Tucker & wf Lucy, formerly Lucy Eckles; and William Basebeech and wf Patsey, formerly Patsey Eckles.

*NOTE: The Tabitha Tucker, formerly Tabitha Eckles, is wife of Paschal Tucker, son of Matthew Tucker (II).*

*NOTE: The Matthew Tucker who md Lucy Eckles is Matthew Tucker (III), son of Mathew Tucker (II).*

*NOTE: It is difficult to know if the following land patents and grant apply to any of this family of Matthew Tuckers. Matthew Tucker (I) who lived in Amelia Co,. until 1785, may have patented land in 1756 and 1767, but probably not in 1784. Matthew Tucker (II) was not born until 1736 and was only 20 in 1756, but he may have patented land in 1767 and 1784. Matthew Tucker (III) was probably not born until 1767. These patents most probably belonged to the Matthew Tucker of another family. The patents are listed here only for future reference.*

ALBEMARLE CO., VA.

Patent 33-165, Matthew Tucker, 16 Aug 1756, Albemarle Co., 378 ac. Hardware Ri.

AMHEARST CO., VA.

Patent 37-124, Matthew Tucker, 10 Sep 1767, Amhearst Co., 2 ac., b.s. Buffalo Ri.

Grant M-478, Matthew Tucker, 28 Oct 1784, Amhearst Co., 116 ac. br. of Dutch Cr.

> *NOTE: It has recently come to the attention of this compiler that the above patents and grant pertain to a Matthew Tucker who d. in Campbell Co, and who was son of Drury Tucker, who was son of John Tucker & 1st wf Catharine, who was son of Francis Tucker (c1668-1723). The John Tucker who m 1st Catharine was the same John Tucker who m 2nd Ann Tally, and the brother of Matthew Tucker I. This has not been verified by this compiler.*

SUMMARY:

Matthew Tucker (II) b ca 1736, son of Matthew Tucker Sr (I) of Pr. Geo. & Amelia Counties, lived in the area of Amelia Co. which was formed into Nottoway Co. in 1789, died 1817 Nottoway Co., md 1st before 1765 Rachael ___, d before 1788, md 2nd 1788 Elizabeth Rease, and had issue:

Paschal Tucker (son of Rachael), b ca 1765, d 1805, md 1787 Tabitha Eckles, dau of Thomas Eckles, & had no issue.

Tabitha Eckles Tucker md 2nd Joseph Moon.

Matthew Tucker Jr (III) (son of Rachael) b ca 1767, d 1833, md Lucy Eckles, dau of Thomas Eckles.

Harbert (or Herbert) Tucker (son of Rachael) b ca 1777, d ca 1816, md Elizabeth (probably Elizabeth Eckles, dau of James Eckles Sr).

Llewellyn Tucker md Jane Moon.

Dicey Tucker.

Susanah Tucker md ____ Clardy, & had issue: Polly Clardy, Milly Clardy, Elizabeth Clardy md Burwell Hudgins.

Nancy Tucker md ____ Bevill.

Elizabeth (Betsy) Tucker md 1787 Edward Eckles son of Thomas Eckles.

Delphia (Philadelphia) Tucker md 1786 Isham Eckles, son of Thomas Eckles.

Letty (Lucy) Tucker md Abraham Stow.

Rachel Tucker md Carter Hudgings.

# T0151100 - PASCHAL TUCKER

## MD TABITHA ECKLES

## SON OF MATTHEW TUCKER JR-SR (the 2ND)

## MD 1ST RACHAEL \_\_\_,
## MD 2ND ELIZABETH \_\_\_

AMELIA CO. VA.

LIST OF TITHABLES

| | | |
|---|---|---|
| 1781 | | Pascall Tucker listed as 16-yr-up tithable in household of his father Matthew Tucker. |
| 1785 | 1 | Pascal Tucker |
| 1787 | | Parskill Tucker listed in household of Matthew Tucker |
| 1788 | 1 | Parschal Tucker. |

MARRIAGE BONDS

22 Dec 1787, Paschal Tucker to Tabitha Eckles, Security Edward Eckles, Parent Thomas Eckles.

NOTTOWAY CO. VA.

1789 Nottoway Co. was formed from Amelia Co.

LAND TAX RECORDS

1804-1813 Paschal Tucker 100 ac. Hurricane Cr.

DB 2-436, 31 Aug 1803, Matthew Tucker Senr to Paschal Tucker, both of Nottoway Co., for love & good will, gift of 100 ac., on Hurricane Swamp, bo. Cates, Leonard, Thos. Eckles, Stephen Hightower, Cryer. S/ Matthew x Tucker, Wit: Saunders Crenshaw, James Eckles, Truman Eckles.

WB 2-163, wp 6 Jun 1805, will of Paschal Tucker of Nottoway Co.
Leg: wife Tabitha - use of estate for life.
Nephew Joel Tucker (son of my brother Matthew Tucker) - all my land.
Niece Sally Echols (dau. of Edward Echols).
Exec: wife Tabitha & friend Freeman Echols.

Wit: Ephram Echols, Joel Echols, James Echols. S/ Paschal Tucker.

WB 2-281, 5 Jun 1806, Inv. of Paschal Tucker, by Tabitha Tucker & Freeman Echols. Included negro woman Mary.

*NOTE: Paschal Tucker was a witness to the will of his grandfather Matthew Tucker Sr (I). (Amelia Co. WB 3-291, dated 3 Mar 1784).*

*NOTE: Matthew Tucker Sr (II), in Nottoway Co WB 4-63, dated 1810, probated 1817, did not name his son Paschal as a legatee, because Paschal had already died in 1805. Paschal was first listed as a 16-yr-up tithable in the household of his father in Amelia Co. in 1781, so he must have been born ca 1765 as the son of Matthew Tucker Jr-Sr (II) & 1st wife Rachael.*

*NOTE: The will of Paschal Tucker (Nottoway Co. WB 2-163, probated 6 Jun 1805), identifies a "nephew Joel Tucker, as son of my brother Matthew Tucker". It appears then that Paschal Tucker was a half-brother of Matthew Tucker (III) and son of Matthew Tucker (II), (1736-1817) and grandson of Matthew Tucker (I), (1699-1785).*

OB 10-100, 3 Jan 1828, Anderson Vaughan & wf Sally, formerly Sally Eckles, John W. Tucker & Asa Tucker children of Joel Tucker decd, infants of tender years by Ann Tucker their next friend -vs- Asa B. Winn, Adm. of Tabitha Moon decd formerly Tucker - commissioners divided slaves belonging to est. of Paschal Tucker decd into two parts according to his will, allotting to heirs of Joel Tucker decd one part -- & to Anderson Vaughan & wf Sally one part.

SUMMARY:

Paschal Tucker, son of Matthew Tucker, Jr-Sr (II) & 1st wife Rachael _____, b ca 1765 in Amelia Co., d 1805 in Nottoway Co., md 1787 Tabitha Eckles, dau. of Thomas Eckles and had no issue.

Tabitha Eckles Tucker, widow of Paschal Tucker, d before 1828, md 2nd after 1805 Joseph Moon.

# T0151200 - MATTHEW TUCKER (III)

## MD LUCY ECKLES

## SON OF MATTHEW TUCKER JR-SR (II)

## MD 1ST RACHAEL ___,
## MD 2ND ELIZABETH ECKLES ___

NOTTOWAY CO., VA.

WB 2-163, wd 6 Mar 1805, wp 6 Jun 1805, will of Paschal Tucker of Nottoway Co. Va. named:
wife Tabitha - all real & personal estate for life.
nephew Joel Tucker (son of my brother Matthew Tucker) all my land, plus 2/3 of increase of two female negroes Mary & Annaca.
Niece Sally Eckles (dau. of Edwd Eckles) -- 1/3 of increase of negroes Mary & Annaca.
At death of wife, balance of estate to Nephew Joel Tucker & Niece Sally Eckles.
Exor: wife Tabitha & friend Freeman Eckles. S/ Paschal Tucker. Wit: Ephraim Eckles, Joel Eckles, James Eckles.

WB 2-328, wd 22 Aug 1806, wp ____ Jul 1807, will of Phebe Tucker of Nottoway Co., names:
Bro. Matthew Tucker, negro woman named Isabell & all her increase.
Milly Branch Clardy - dovetail chest.
Exor: ____ Crenshaw & Thomas Eckols. S/ Phebe x Tucker. Wit: Alain Crenshaw, Judith Crenshaw.

WB 4-63, wd 11 Jan 1810, wp 5 Jun 1817. will of Matthew Tucker Senr. of Nottoway Co.,
Son Matthew Tucker - the land whereon he now lives & bo. by land of Bottom Stegall & including all the land I bought of Charles Anderson, but no part of the land I bought of Bottom Stegall.
Son Lewellen Tucker - L44. in addition to what I have already advanced for him.
Wife, (not named) for life or widowhood, best male slaves I have, best horse, best feather bed, furniture & priviledge of living where

I now live & making a reasonable use of my plantation to support her & her property.

Dau. Dicey - one feather bed & furniture as good as those given to my other daughters. (not named)

Son Harbert - all rest of my land subject to provision made for my wife.

I relinquish all claim to negro woman Milley which my wife brought with her.

Balance of estate to be equally divided btwn all my children, and three daughters of my daughter Susanah Clardy be considered as one of my children & entitled to one share to be equally divided btwn them when they marry or come of lawful age.

Exors: friends Saml Morgan, Richard Epes, Saunders Crenshaw & my son Harbert Tucker. S/ Matthew x Tucker Senr. Wit: Saml G. Williams, Thomas Morgan, Thomas Fitzgerald.

CODICIL, 26 Jul 1816, Whereas son Harbert Tucker has died & left widow & five children, I give to those five children all that part of my estate which I had given to their father, equally divided btwn them, reserving enjoyment of same to my son's widow for life or widowhood. S/ Matthew x Tucker.

Wit: William Crenshaw, Joseph W. Crenshaw, Saml Morgan.

Order Book 5-167, 5 Jul 1807 identifies legatees of Thomas Eckles as: Isham Eckles executor; Joel Eckles; Charnel Hightower & wf Salley, formerly Salley Eckles; George Turner & wf Elizabeth, formerly Elizabeth Eckles; Edward Eckles; Francis Eckles; Thomas Eckles; Tabitha Tucker, formerly Tabitha Eckles; Joel Eckles & wf Polly, formerly Polly Eckles; Matthew Tucker & wf Lucy, formerly Lucy Eckles; and William Basebeech and wf Patsey, formerly Patsey Eckles.

Order Book 8-84, 4 Dec 1817, Matthew Tucker, Isham Eckles & wf Delphia, Edward Eckles & wf Elizabeth, Abraham Stow & wf Letty, Lewelling Tucker, Nancy Bovill, Elizabeth Tucker, Carter Hudgings & wf Rachel, Dicey Tucker, Polly Clardy, Milly Clardy and Burwell Hudgins and wf Elizabeth -vs- Samuel Morgan Sheriff - - decreed & ordered to divide estate of Matthew Tucker

Senr decd according to residuary clause in his will disposing of balance of his estate.

Order Book 8-265, 6 Mar 1819,Matthew Tucker, Isham Eckles & wf Delphia, Edward Eckles & wf Elizabeth, Abraham Stow & wf Letty, Lewelling Tucker, Nancy Bovill, Elizabeth Tucker, Carter Hudgings & wf Rachel, Dicey Tucker, Polly Clardy, Milly Clardy & Burwell Hudgings & wf Elizabeth -vs- Bartlett P. Todd deputy Sheriff - commissioners divided into 10 parts, the property slaves of Matthew Tucker decd: Bob, Isabel, Patram, Ralph, Eliza, Mary & her son Peter, Hall, Sam, Ellick, Amy & Patrick, & assigned 1/10th part each to Nancy Beville, Mrs. Susanna Clardy's heirs, Edward Eckles & wf Elizabeth, Matthew Tucker Jr, Lewelling Tucker, Mrs. Elizabeth Tucker widow of Herbert Tucker decd, Dicy Tucker, Isham Eckles & wf Delphia, Abraham Stow & wf Letty, Carter Hudgings & wf Rachel.

WB 6-424, wd 4 Dec 1827, wp 7 Nov 1833, will of Matthew Tucker of Nottoway Co.
Dau. Susan Goulder - 1 feather bed & furniture.
Wife Lucy - for life, bal. of personal & real estate consisting of land on which I now live, my negroes, stock of every kind household furniture & crop now on plantation, after my debts are paid.
Son Thomas - after wife's death, tract of land mentioned, with all appurtenances thereto.
to John W Tucker & Asa Tucker, orphans of my son Joel Tucker decd, $20. each, after wife's death.
After wife's death, bal. of est., after specific legacies above, equally divided among my children: Thomas Tucker, Martha Ellington, Susan Goulder & grand daughter Eliza Clardy. S/ Matthew x Tucker. Wit: Asa Cranshaw, Joel Eckles, Spencer G. Tucker.

Order Book 11-140, 5 Dec 1833, Thomas Tucker, George Goulder & wf Susan formerly Tucker, & John Ellington & wf Patsey formerly Tucker -vs- Elizabeth Clardy by Wm. Crenshaw her guardian ad litum. Wm. Crenshaw is appointed guardian of defendant (Elizabeth Clardy). Court appointed commissioners to divide the negroes of which Matthew Tucker decd possessed, btwn Thomas Tucker, George Goulder & wf Susan, John E. Ellington & wf Patsey & Eliza Clardy.

Order Book 11-145, 2 Jan 1834. Court doth assign Thomas Tucker, Guardian to Eliza Clardy, orphan of Benjamin Clardy decd.

Order Book 11-240, 7 May 1835 -- this detailed order -- includes the heirs of Matthew Tucker Jr, as: John Ellington & wf Martha, Thomas Tucker, George Goulder & wf Susan, Elizabeth Clardy, only child of Holly Tucker, John W. & Asa Tucker, infant children of Joel Tucker.

> *NOTE: When Paschal Tucker wrote his will in 1805 (WB 2-163), he named his nephew Joel Tucker son of his brother Matthew Tucker (III). Matthew Tucker (III) in his will written in 1827 named John W & Asa Tucker as orphan children of his son Joel Tucker. In 1824 (OB 9-118), Ann Tucker was referred to as administrator of est of Joel Tucker decd. Since Joel Tucker had two sons prior to his death in 1824, he was most probably age 21 and married c1821 and therefore born c1800. If Joel was b c1800, his father Matthew Tucker (III) was probably age 21 and married c1789, and therefore b c1768. If Matthew Tucker (III) was b c1768, then he was most probably the second son of his father Matthew Tucker Sr (II) (1736-1817) & 1st wf Rachael.*

SUMMARY:

Matthew Tucker Jr (III), son of Matthew Tucker Sr (II) & probably his 1st wf Rachael ___, b c1768 in Amelia Co., d 1833 in Nottoway Co., md c1789 probably in Amelia Co. Lucy Eckles dau of Thomas Eckles, & had issue:

Joel Tucker, b c1800, md c1821 ?Ann ____ , died 1824, leaving orphan sons:

John W. Tucker b c1822
Asa Tucker b c1823.

Thomas Tucker probably b c1802.

Holly Tucker, md prior to 1833 Benjamin Clardy, & had issue:

Elizabeth Clardy b prior to 1833

Martha (Patsey) Tucker, md prior to 1833 John Ellington.

Susan Tucker, md prior to 1833 George Goulder.

# T0151210 - JOEL TUCKER

## SON OF MATTHEW TUCKER (III)
## MD LUCY ECKLES

NOTTOWAY CO., VA.

WB 2-163, wd 6 Mar 1805, wp 6 Jun 1805, will of Paschal Tucker of Nottoway Co. Va. named:
wife Tabitha - all real & personal estate for life.
nephew Joel Tucker (son of my brother Matthew Tucker) all my land, plus 2/3 of increase of two female negroes Mary & Annaca.
Niece Sally Eckles (dau. of Edwd Eckles) -- 1/3 of increase of negroes Mary & Annaca.
At death of wife, balance of estate to Nephew Joel Tucker & Niece Sally Eckles.
Exor: wife Tabitha & friend Freeman Eckles. S/ Paschal Tucker.
Wit: Ephraim Eckles, Joel Eckles, James Eckles.

OB 9-118, 6 Aug 1824, Joel Tucker assee of Joseph Sheffield -vs-Francis L. Moseley, suit in the name of Ann Tucker admin of Joel Tucker decd. Judgment $36.00.

> *NOTE: From above order, it appears Joel Tucker d ca 1824. Was Ann Tucker the wife of Joel Tucker? See OB 10-100 in which Ann Tucker is referred to as next friend of John W. & Asa Tucker, orphan sons of Joel Tucker.*

OB 9-322, 6 Oct 1825, Ann L. Tucker, adm of est. of Joel Tucker decd, continued.

WB 6-424, wd 4 Dec 1827, wp 7 Nov 1833, will of Matthew Tucker of Nottoway Co.
Dau. Susan Goulder - 1 feather bed & furniture.
Wife Lucy - for life, bal. of personal & real estate consisting of land on which I now live, my negroes, stock of every kind household furniture & crop now on plantation, after my debts are paid.
Son Thomas - after wife's death, tract of land mentioned, with all appurtenances thereto.

to John W Tucker & Asa Tucker, orphans of my son Joel Tucker decd, $20. each, after wife's death.

After wife's death, bal. of est., after specific legacies above, equally divided among my children: Thomas Tucker, Martha Ellington, Susan Goulder & grand daughter Eliza Clardy. S/ Matthew x Tucker. Wit: Asa Cranshaw, Joel Eckles, Spencer G. Tucker.

OB 10-100, 3 Jan 1828, Anderson Vaughan & wf Sally, formerly Sally Eckles, John W. Tucker & Asa Tucker, children of Joel Tucker decd, infants of tender years by Ann Tucker their next friend -vs- Asa Winm adm. of Tabitha Moon decd formerly Tucker - Commissioners appointed to divide slaves belonging to est. of Paschal Tucker decd in two parts according to his will, alloting one part to heirs of Joel Tucker decd, and one part to Anderson Vaughan & wf Sally.

> NOTE: See WB 2-163 will of Paschal Tucker in which he left balance of est. to nephew Joel Tucker & neice Sally Echles, dau of Edward Eckles - who now had md Anderson Vaughan. See OB 9-118 in which Ann Tucker is administrator of Joel Tucker. Does next friend mean next of kin? Was Ann the wife of Joel & mother of John W. & Asa Tucker?

OB 10-243, 6 Feb 1829, Thomas T Tucker is appointed Guardian of John W. Tucker & Asa Tucker orphans of Joel Tucker. Thomas Spain & Matthew Tucker, surety.

OB 10-393, 2 Dec 1830, Daniel J. Jackson is appointed guardian of John W. Tucker and Asa Tucker, orphans of Joel Tucker decd. John J. Gimmer & Peterson W. Harper, securities.

OB ___ -231, 5 Feb 1835, John W. Tucker & Asa E. Tucker infants & sole legatees of Joel Tucker decd, by James S. Jeter their next friend, -vs- Daniel J. Jackson guardian of John W. Tucker & Asa E. Tucker, by consent of parties - court ordered Peterson W. Harper to sell to highest bidder the 105 ac. of land on a credit of 12 months.

*NOTE: See WB 2-163, in which Paschal Tucker willed all his land to nephew Joel Tucker. See Land Tax Record 1804-13, in which Paschal Tucker held 100 ac. on Hurricane Cr.*

*NOTE: When Paschal Tucker wrote his will in 1805 (WB 2-163), he named his nephew Joel Tucker son of his brother Matthew Tucker (III). Matthew Tucker (III) in his will written in 1827 named John W & Asa Tucker as orphan children of his son Joel Tucker. In 1824 (OB 9-118), Ann Tucker was referred to as administrator of est of Joel Tucker decd. Since Joel Tucker had two sons prior to his death in 1824, he was most probably age 21 and married ca 1821 and therefore born ca 1800. If Joel was b ca 1800, his father Matthew Tucker (III) was probably age 21 and married ca 1789, and therefore b ca 1768. If Matthew Tucker (III) was b ca 1768, then he was most probably the second son of his father Matthew Tucker Sr (II) (1736-1817) & 1st wf Rachael.*

SUMMARY:

Joel Tucker son of Matthew Tucker (III) & wf Lucy Eckles, b ca 1800 in Nottoway Co., d 1824 in Nottoway Co., md ca 1821 probably in Nottoway Co. ?Ann _?_, & had issue:

John W. Tucker b ca 1822.

Asa Tucker b ca 1823.

# T0151220 - THOMAS TUCKER

## SON OF MATTHEW TUCKER JR (III)

### MD LUCY ECKLES

OB 10-243, 6 Feb 1829, Thomas T. Tucker is appointed Guardian of John W. Tucker & Asa Tucker orphans of Joel Tucker. Thomas Spain & Matthew Tucker, surety.

*NOTE: Thomas T. Tucker was at least age 21 in 1829, when appointed Guardian of his orphaned nephews, so he was b before 1808.*

OB 10-393, 2 Dec 1830, Daniel J. Jackson is appointed guardian of John W. Tucker and Asa Tucker, orphans of Joel Tucker decd. John J. Gimmer & Peterson W. Harper, securities.

NOTTOWAY CO., VA.

WB 6-424, wd 4 Dec 1827, wp 7 Nov 1833, will of Matthew Tucker of Nottoway Co.
Dau. Susan Goulder - 1 feather bed & furniture.
Wife Lucy - for life, bal. of personal & real estate consisting of land on which I now live, my negroes, stock of every kind household furniture & crop now on plantation, after my debts are paid.
Son Thomas - after wife's death, tract of land mentioned, with all appurtenances thereto.
John W Tucker & Asa Tucker, orphans of my son Joel Tucker decd, $20. each, after wife's death.
After wife's death, bal. of est., after specific legacies above, equally divided among my children: Thomas Tucker, Martha Ellington, Susan Goulder & grand daughter Eliza Clardy.
Exor: son Thomas Tucker.
S/ Matthew x Tucker. Wit: Asa Cranshaw, Joel Eckles, Spencer G. Tucker.

OB 11-126, 7 Nov 1833, will of Matthew Tucker decd ordered recorded & Thomas T. Tucker executor took oath & acknowledged bond. Ordered any three of Edward Farley, Asa Hawkes, George

W. Clark & Caleb D. Pollard duly sworn to appraise personal & real est of Matthew Tucker decd.

Order Book 11-140, 5 Dec 1833, Thomas Tucker, George Goulder & wf Susan formerly Tucker, & John Ellington & wf Patsey formerly Tucker -vs- Elizabeth Clardy by Wm. Crenshaw her guardian ad litum. Wm. Crenshaw is appointed guardian of defendant (Elizabeth Clardy). Court appointed commissioners to divide the negroes of which Matthew Tucker decd possessed, btwn Thomas Tucker, George Goulder & wf Susan, John E. Ellington & wf Patsey & Eliza Clardy.

Order Book 11-145, 2 Jan 1834. Court doth assign Thomas Tucker, Guardian to Eliza Clardy, orphan of Benjamin Clardy decd.

SUMMARY:

Thomas Tucker, son of Matthew Tucker (III) & wf Lucy Eckles, b before 1808, d ___

# T0151300 - HARBERT TUCKER

## (or HERBERT)

## MD ELIZABETH _____

## SON OF MATTHEW TUCKER JR-SR (II)
## MD 1ST RACHAEL _____,
## MD 2ND ELIZABETH_____

NOTTOWAY CO., VA.

DB 3-222, 10 Dec 1798, rec 1 Jan 1807, Charles Anderson & wf Mary to Matthew Tucker Jr of Nottoway Co., for L9., 20 ac., bo. Steagal, Griggs. Wit: Herbert Tucker, Thos. Echols, Paschal Tucker. Proved 5 Sep 1799. Oath of Thomas Echols & Herbert Tucker, Paschal Tucker decd.

*NOTE: Herbert Tucker was at least age 21 in 1798 when he witnessed a deed of his father, so he would have been born by 1777. Although this deed was written in 1798, & proved in 1799, it was not recorded until 1807.*

*NOTE: There were several marriages between the Tucker and Eckles families. Herbert Tucker probably married Elizabeth Eckles, dau of James Eckles Sr, probably c1798, probably in Nottoway Co.*

W8 3-___, wd 8 Oct 1815, wp 6 Jun 1816, will of James Eckles Sr., names sons James, Ephriam, Joel, Freeman; daughters Patsey Eckles, Bethiah River, Priscilla Hightower, Elizabeth Tucker. Wit: William River, Thomas Eckles, Sam'l Morgan.

WB 4-63, wd 11 Jan 1810, wp 5 Jun 1817. will of Matthew Tucker Senr. of Nottoway Co., names: Son Matthew Tucker - Son Lewellen Tucker - Wife, (not named) - Dau. Dicey - one feather bed & furniture as good as those given to my other daughters. (not named) - Son Harbert - all rest of my land subject to provision made for my wife. - Exors: friends Saml Morgan, Richard Epes, Saunders Crenshaw & my son Harbert Tucker. -

CODICIL, 26 Jul 1816, Whereas son Harbert Tucker has died & left widow & five children, I give to those five children all that part of my estate which I had given to their father, equally divided btwn them, reserving enjoyment of same to my son's widow for life or widowhood.

*NOTE: From above codicil, Harbert (or Herbert) Tucker d 1816.*

Order Book 8-48, 2 Oct 1817, Elizabeth Tucker is appointed special Guardian to the orphans of Harbert Tucker decd.

Order Book 8-48, 2 Oct 1817, Elizabeth Tucker widow and relict of Matthew Tucker Senr decd -vs- Matthew Tucker & Elizabeth Tucker, and Patsey E. Tucker, Spencer G. Tucker, Elizabeth A. Tucker, Matthew J. Tucker and Joshua G. Tucker, infants of tender years by Elizabeth Tucker their Guardian - - ordered that Samuel Morgan, Samuel B. Deter, Bartelot P. Todd, Joel Eckles and Richard Epes or any three of them, attended by a competent surveyor, do lay off, allot & assign to complainant, one third part of land of Matthew Tucker Senr late, to hold as her dower.

*NOTE: The above identifies the 5 children of Matthew Tucker as Patsey (Martha) E., Spencer G., Elizabeth A., Matthew J., & Joshua G. Tucker, probably in the order of birth.*

Order Book 8-265, 6 Mar 1819, Matthew Tucker, Isham Eckles & wf Delphia, Edward Eckles & wf Elizabeth, Abraham Stow & wf Letty, Lewelling Tucker, Nancy Bevill, Elizabeth Tucker, Carter Hudgings & wf Rachel, Dicey Tucker, Polly Clardy, Milly Clardy & Burwell Hudgings & wf Elizabeth -vs- Bartlett P. Todd deputy Sheriff - commissioners divided into 10 parts, the property slaves of Matthew Tucker decd: Bob, Isabel, Patram, Ralph, Eliza, Mary & her son Peter, Hall, Sam, Ellick, Amy & Patrick, & assigned 1/10th part each to Nancy Beville, Mrs. Susanna Clardy's heirs, Edward Eckles & wf Elizabeth, Matthew Tucker Jr, Lewelling Tucker, Mrs. Elizabeth Tucker widow of Herbert Tucker decd, Dicy Tucker, Isham Eckles & wf Delphia, Abraham Stow & wf Letty, Carter Hudgings & wf Rachel.

Order Book 8-411, 2 Feb 1820, Martha E. Tucker, orphan of Herbert Tucker decd, made choice of Kennon Spain for her

Guardian, and thereupon sd Spain with Joel Eckles & Thomas Eckles his securities entered bond of $1,800.

*NOTE: Martha E. Tucker probably was age 16 in 1820 when she chose her guardian, so she was probably b c1804.*

Order Book 9-103, 5 Aug 1824, An acct of Elizabeth Tucker Jr as administratrix of Herbert Tucker, decd with a report of commissioners thereon, recorded.

*NOTE: It appears that Elizabeth Tucker widow of Herbert Tucker, is frequently referred to as Elizabeth Tucker Jr, to distinguish her from her mother-in-law Elizabeth Tucker widow of Matthew Tucker Jr-Sr (2nd), who is referred to as Elizabeth Tucker Sr.*

Order Book 5(9?)-227, 5 Aug 1824, Est of Herbert Tucker decd to Elizabeth Tucker Jr, Administratrix. Cash paid to Wood Jones, James Cabaniss, B. P. Todd, Matthew Tucker, Hartwell Spain, John A. Hatchett, Elizabeth Tucker, Jno Cabaniss, James Williams, Carter Hudgings, James Eckles Jr., James Williams, David Kenady, Thomas Eckles, Bridgforth & Burton, William T. Wills. Total $629.88.

Order Book 10-179, 7 Nov 1828. Certificate is granted to Hartwell Spain for obtaining letters of administration on the estate of Elizabeth Tucker Jr, decd, & ordered that Asa Crenshaw, Allen Crenshaw, William Crenshaw, Asa B. Winn & Henry C. Worsham appraise the estate of Elizabeth Tucker Jr decd.

*NOTE: It appears from the above that Elizabeth Tucker Jr, widow of Herbert Tucker, died in 1828.*

Order Book 10-185, 7 Nov 1828. Kennon Spain & wf Martha E. formerly Tucker, and Spencer Tucker -vs- Matthew J. Tucker & Joshua G. Tucker infant children of Elizabeth Tucker decd, by Hartwell Spain their Special Guardian. -- commissioners appointed to sell negro man, property of Elizabeth Tucker decd & assign proceeds in equal parts to Kennon Spain & wf Martha E, Spencer G. Tucker, Matthew J. Tucker & Joshua G. Tucker.

*NOTE: From above, Martha E. Tucker, dau of Herbert & Elizabeth Tucker, by Nov 1828, had married Kennon Spain whom she had chosen as her guardian in 1820 (see OB 8-411). Hartwell Spain was guardian of Matthew J. & Joshua G. Tucker, who were still infant orphans of Herbert & Elizabeth Tucker. The daughter Elizabeth A. Tucker was no longer named as an heir in the above and the below court orders.*

Order Took 10-258, 4 Jun 1829, Kennon Spain & wf Martha E. formerly Tucker -vs- Spencer G. Tucker & Mathew James Tucker & Joshua G. Tucker infant children of Elizabeth Tucker by H. C. Worsham their special guardian -- commissioners & surveyor to lay off & divide land of Mrs. Elizabeth Tucker decd, in equal parts btwn her children, viz: Kennon Spain & wf Marth E., Spencer G. Tucker, Matthew James Tucker & Joshua G. Tucker.

*NOTE: From above, H. C. Worsham was new guardian of Spencer, Matthew & Joshua Tucker, infant orphans of Herbert & Elizabeth Tucker.*

Order Book 10-292, 1 Oct 1829. Matthew J. Tucker & Joshua G. Tucker, orphans of Herbert Tucker decd, chose Asa Hawkes for their guardian.

*NOTE: From above, it appears that Spencer G. Tucker may have attained age 21 in 1829 & was born probably c1808.*

Order Book 11-143, 2 Jan 1834. Charles Wilson -vs- Spencer Tucker, Matthew J. Tucker, Kennon Spain & wf, & Joshua G. Tucker infant by his guardian Asa Hawkes. Commissioners appointed to sell land of Mrs. Elizabeth Tucker & assign equal parts to Charles J. Wilson, Matthew J. Tucker, Kennon Spain & wf, & Joshua G. Tucker.

*NOTE: The above court order is most confusing. Who was Charles Wilson, and why would he be an heir of an equal share of land of Mrs Elizabeth Tucker widow of Herbert Tucker? Was he the husband of their daughter, Elizabeth A. Tucker, who was named in OB 8-48, 1817, but not named in this order? And why was Spencer Tucker, who was a party to this deed, not assigned an equal part?*

153

*NOTE: From above it appears that Matthew J Tucker had attained age 21 before 1834 and was probably born before 1813.*

OB 11-210, 6 Nov 1834, Joshua G. Tucker, orphan of Herbert Tucker, chose Peterson W. Harper as his guardian.

OB 11-237, 1 Dec 1836. A deed from Joshua G. Tucker to Matthew J. Tucker dated 25 Oct 1836, recd & rec.

*NOTE: From above, Joshua G. Tucker had attained age 21 by 1836, and was probably born c1815.*

SUMMARY:

Herbert Tucker, son of Matthew Tucker (II) & 2nd wf Elizabeth ____, b before 1777 in Amelia Co, d 1816 in Nottoway Co, m ___ Elizabeth Eckles, d 1828, dau of James Eckles Sr, & had issue:

Elizabeth A. Tucker, ? may have m Charles Wilson.

Martha E. (Patsy E.) Tucker b c1804, m 1828 Kennon Spain.

Spencer G. Tucker b c1808, m Elizabeth Eckles, dau of Thomas Eckles.

Matthew James Tucker, b c1813, m Elizabeth Williams dau of Robert C. Williams & wf Susan.

Joshua Gilliam Tucker b c1815, m Henrietta Harper.

# T0151400 - LEWELLING TUCKER

## MD JANE MOON
## SON OF MATTHEW TUCKER JR-SR (II)
## MD 1ST RACHAEL ____ ,
## MD 2ND ELIZABETH ECKLES

NOTTOWAY CO. VA.

WB 4-63, wd 11 Jan 1810, wp 5 Jun 1817. will of Matthew Tucker Senr. of Nottoway Co., names: Son Matthew Tucker - Son Lewellen Tucker - L44. in addition to what I have already advanced for him. - Wife, (not named) - Dau. Dicey - one feather bed & furniture as good as those given to my other daughters. (not named) - Son Harbert - Exors: friends Saml Morgan, Richard Epes, Saunders Crenshaw & my son Harbert Tucker.

Order Book 8-84, 4 Dec 1817, Matthew Tucker, Isham Eckles & wf Delphia, Edward Eckles & wf Elizabeth, Abraham Stow & wf Letty, Lewelling Tucker, Nancy Bovill, Elizabeth Tucker, Carter Hudgings & wf Rachel, Dicey Tucker, Polly Clardy, Milly Clardy and Burwell Hudgins and wf Elizabeth -vs- Samuel Morgan Sheriff - - decreed & ordered to divide estate of Matthew Tucker Senr decd according to residuary clause in his will disposing of balance of his estate.

Order Book 8-265, 6 Mar 1819, Matthew Tucker, Isham Eckles & wf Delphia, Edward Eckles & wf Elizabeth, Abraham Stow & wf Letty, Lewelling Tucker, Nancy Bevill, Elizabeth Tucker, Carter Hudgings & wf Rachel, Dicey Tucker, Polly Clardy, Milly Clardy & Burwell Hudgings & wf Elizabeth -vs- Bartlett P. Todd deputy Sheriff - commissioners divided into 10 parts, the property slaves of Matthew Tucker decd: Bob, Isabel, Patram, Ralph, Eliza, Mary & her son Peter, Hall, Sam, Ellick, Amy & Patrick, & assigned 1/10th part each to Nancy Beville, Mrs. Susanna Clardy's heirs, Edward Eckles & wf Elizabeth, Matthew Tucker Jr, Lewelling, Mrs. Elizabeth Tucker widow of Herbert Tucker decd, Dicy Tucker, Isham Eckles & wf Delphia, Abraham Stow & wf Letty,

Carter Hudgings & wf Rachel.

WB 5-377, 4 May 1821. Examination, state & settle a/c of Matthew Tucker Sr. To all heirs of Matthew Tucker except Lewelling Tucker.

OB 9-356, 2 Feb 1826. A deed from Lewelling Tucker & wf Jane to Samuel P. Jeter produced.

*NOTE: The above indicates that Lewelling Tucker was married before Feb 1826. Since he was a party in his own right to a court order in 1817, he probably was at least age 21 at that time, & probably was born on or before 1796.*

OB 9-457, 5 Oct 1826. Tabitha Moon, widow of Joseph Moon decd, Benjamin Moon, John Moon, Lewelling Tucker & wf Jane formerly Moon, Thomas Moon, Susanna W. Moon, Polly B. Moon, Joseph Moon & James W. Moon -vs- William T. Wills, deputy Sheriff of Nottoway Co. & Adm. of Joseph Moon decd - - divided estate of Joseph Moon decd - Tabitha Moon to pay $40.88 to Lewelling Tucker & wf Jane formerly Moon - -

*NOTE: From above, it appears Lewelling Tucker m Jane Moon, dau. of Joseph Moon & wf Tabitha, who was formerly Tabitha Tucker widow of Paschal Tucker decd, older half-brother of Lewelling, and who was formerly Tabitha Eckles dau of Thomas Eckles.*

OB 10-100, 3 Jan 1828, Anderson Vaughan & wf Sally formerly Sally Eckles, John W. Tucker & Asa Tucker children of Joel Tucker deed, infants of tender years by Ann Tucker their next friend -vs- Asa B. Winn, Adm. of Tabitha Moon decd formerly Tucker - commissioners divided slaves belonging to est. of Paschal Tucker decd into two parts according to his will, allotting to heirs of Joel Tucker decd one part -- & to Anderson Vaughan & wf Sally one part.

*NOTE: By WB 2-163, 1805 Paschal Tucker left personal estate to wife Tabitha (dau of Thomas Eckles) for life, then to nephew Joel Tucker (son of my brother Matthew Tucker) and niece Sally Echols (dau of Edward Echols). From above OB 10-100, it appears that Paschal Tucker's widow Tabitha married 2nd Joseph Moon, who died 1826. Tabitha Moon died 1828. Their dau Jane Moon m Lewelling Tucker, younger half-brother of Paschal Tucker.*

This Lewelling Tucker was not further researched by this compiler.

SUMMARY:

Lewelling Tucker, son of Matthew Tucker Jr-Sr (II) & 2nd wf Elizabeth _?_, b c1796, d _?_, m before 1826 Jane Moon, dau of Joseph Moon & wf Tabitha.

*Tabitha Moon was formerly widow of Paschal Tucker (older half-brother of Lewelling) & dau of Thomas Eckles, & sister of Lucy Eckles who m Matthew Tucker (III) (older half-brother of Lewelling).*

*In other words, Lewelling Tucker m the dau. of his former sister-in-law Tabitha, who was also neice of his sister-in-law Lucy.*

# T0152000 - THOMAS TUCKER SR

## MD 1ST LUCY _____,
## MD 2ND MARY COLEMAN
## SON OF MATTHEW TUCKER SR. (I)
## MD MARY _____

AMELIA CO. VA.

WB 3-291, will of Matthew Tucker Sr., wd 3 Mar 1784, *(wp not shown - See WB 3-357.)*,
names:
dau. Phoebe Tucker - negro Isbell, 5 head cattle, bed & furn.,
for life, then to son Matthew Tucker.
son Thomas Tucker - plantation whereon I now live.
son Henry Tucker - the part of land now in his possession.
Ex: son Matthew Tucker, and Absolom Tucker.
Wit: Absolom Tucker, Joseph Bevill (?), Paschal Tucker.
S/ Matthew Tucker.

WB 3-357, Est. I&A, Matthew Tucker, decd, 20 Jun 1785, by Evans Mitchell, Joseph Bevill, John Morgan.

*NOTE: It is assumed Matthew Tucker Sr. died in 1785.*

LIST OF TITHABLES

| 1755-56 | | Thomas Tucker listed as 16-yr-up tithable in household of his father Matthew Tucker Sr (I). |
|---|---|---|
| 1762 | 1-0 | Thomas Tucker |
| 1763 | 1-0 | Thomas Tucker |
| 1765 | 1-0 | Thomas Tucker |
| 1767 | 1-80 | Thomas Tucker |
| 1769 | 1-84 | Thomas Tucker |
| 1770 | 1-84 | Thomas Tucker |

PERSONAL TAX RECORDS

1782  3  Thomas Tucker, William Edmunds, Bob
1783  3  Thomas Tucker
1786  2  Thomas Tucker

## PERSONAL TAX RECORDS

1787  1  Thomas Tucker
1788  1  Thomas Tucker
1789  1  Thomas Tucker
1790  1  Thomas Tucker
1791  1  Thomas Tucker, Nelson Tucker
   *(See WB 6-128, 1800, Thomas Tucker)*.

## LAND TAX RECORDS

1782        Thomas Tucker, 142 ac.
1787        Alterations - Matthew Tucker Jr by Henry Tucker 50 ac.,
            by Tho. Tucker 50 ac.
1788-90   Thomas Tucker 142 + 60 = 202 ac.
1791-94   Thomas Tucker 202 ac.
1795-99   Thomas Tucker Sr 202 ac.
1800-01   Thomas Tucker Est 202 ac.
1802-07   Thomas Tucker Est 184 ac.
1808-10   Thomas Tucker Est 139 1/4 ac.
1811-17   Thomas Tucker Est 98 3/4 ac. adj. Elizabeth Kidd & John

*NOTE: The 1787 alterations are confusing. Matthew Tucker Sr. owned 100 ac. at time of his will, and gave to son Thomas plantation whereon I live, and to son Henry - land in his possession. The intent of the alteration is probably that Matthew Jr as executor, passed 50 ac. to Thomas and 50 ac. to Henry. This is probably the same as 60 ac. shown in 1788-90.*

*NOTE: The subject Thomas Tucker was first listed as a 16-yr-up tithable in the household of his father Matthew Tucker Sr (the I) in 1755-56, and listed as a separate household in 1762. So he was probably born c1739, age 16 in 1755, and age 21 in 1760.*

DB 9-44, 16 Aug 1766, Peter Coleman Sen to Thomas Tucker, for L26.5., 80 ac., bo. Tucker's Br., joining Michael Clandy & Thomas Berry, William Coleman, Peter Coleman, Henry Tucker, Matthew Tucker Senr. Wit: Thomas Berry, John Hood, Matthew x Tucker. Rec. 25 Sep 1766. S/ Peter Coleman, Martha Coleman.

159

DB 9-302, 25 Apr 1768, Thomas Berry & wf Catherine to Thomas Tucker, for 30 sh., 3 ac., bo. Tucker's Br. on sd Thomas Berry, Matthew Tucker. Wit: Hezekiah Bevill, Robert Sevin, Daniel Allen. Rec. 28 Apr 1768. S/ Thomas Berry, Catherine x Berry.

DB 12-44, 19 Mar 1773, Hezekiah Bevill & wf Ann to Thomas Tucker, for L80., 100 ac. on e.s. Tucker's Br. & joining sd Thomas Tucker, Francis Coleman, George Kidd, Abram Coleman & George Worsham. Wit: John Forham, George Worsham, Henry x Tucker. Rec. 22 Apr 1773. S/ Hezekiah Bevill, Ann Bevil.

DB 12-163, 2 Nov 1773, Thomas Tucker to Henry Tucker for L20., 42 ac., bo. Peter Coleman, Francis Coleman, Matthew Tucker Sen, Henry Tucker. Wit: Thomas Hood, Henry Hall, John Hood Sen. Rec. 25 Nov 1773. Wife Lucy reling. dower. S/ Thomas x Tucker, Lucy x Tucker.

WB 6-128, 25 Sep 1800, I&A Est. of Thomas Tucker. Included negro man Bob, horses, cattle & household furniture & farm tools. Appr: Daniel Allen Sr., Richard Allen, William Coleman Sr. Ex: John Epps. Justice of the Peace, Rice Newman.

> *NOTE: It appears Thomas Tucker died in 1800 without a will, leaving an est. of 202 ac. This est. was distributed among his widow and children, whose names and inheritance are difficult to determine without a will.*

> *NOTE: The Nelson Tucker shown as a 16-yr-up tithable in the household of Thomas Tucker in 1791, was probably his son, b ca1775.*

> *NOTE: Since Thomas Tucker was listed as Sr in the Land Tax of 1795-99, he had a son named Thomas Jr, b c1779.*

MARRIAGES [1]

28 Mar 1792, William Roberts m Rebecc Tucker. Sur. Thomas Hood. p R-3.

23 Jan 1793, Thomas Tucker m Miny (or Mary) Coleman, Sec. Evan Mitchell.

24 Apr 1799, Nelson Tucker m Rhoda Hood, Sec. Solomon Hood.

28 Dec 1799, Edward Hood m Phoebe Tucker, Sur. Abram Hood, m 2 Jan 1800 by Rev. Walthall Robertson who says Phebe. p H-3.

13 Aug 1800, Thomas Tucker m Elizabeth Coleman, Sec. Martin Chandler, Parent John Jones.

*NOTE: The marriage in 1793 is the second marriage of Thomas Tucker Sr; the marriage in 1800 is that of Thomas Tucker Jr, as evidenced by the following deeds.*

DB 21-154, 20 Mar 1801, rec 22 Oct 1801, Nelson Tucker & wf Rhoda, Edward Hood, & Thomas Tucker, to Wm. Coleman, for L18, 18 ac. (no significant bounds). S/ Nelson x Tucker, Rhoda x Tucker, Thomas Tucker, Rebecker x Roberots. Wit: Wm. Coleman, Jasper x Kidd, Archer Coleman.

*NOTE: Why "Rebecker Roberots" would sign this deed instead of Edward Hood is a mystery. It appears that the grantor parties to this deed, e.i. Nelson Tucker, Edward Hood, Thomas Tucker and possibly Rebeccah Roberts were heirs of Thomas Tucker Sr, & they sold a part of his est of 202 ac. 18 ac. = 184 ac. (See Land Tax Record)*

DB 22-403, 27 Apr 1807, Thomas Tucker & wf Elizabeth to William Coleman, for L35.14.1, 19 3/4 ac., being a part of the land sd Tucker lives on which was left him by his father Thomas Tucker decd on s.s. of the road, bo Elizabeth Coleman, John Wells, the road. S/ Thomas Tucker, Elizabeth Tucker. Wit: Archer Coleman, John Clay, Archer Bevil', Robert Bevil', Braxton Coleman.

DB 22-414. 26 Jul 1807, rec 26 Aug 1807, Thomas Tucker to John Clay, for L9., 10 ac., being a part of the tract of land formerly belonging to Thomas Tucker decd, now in possession of Mary Tucker, on s.s. of the long branch, bo Kidd. S/ Thomas x Tucker. Wit: Robert Clay, William Clay, Jesse Clay, James H. Mumford.

*NOTE: Mary Tucker is apparently the 2nd wf of Thomas Tucker Sr. per deeds above and below.*

DB 22-448, 15 Aug 1806, rec 1808, Thomas Tucker to John Eppes, for $91., 15 ac., being a part of the land he now lives on which was left him by his father Thomas Tucker Sen decd, on b.s. of Hood's Road, bo. John Eppes, Mary Tucker's dower line, former property of Abraham Coleman now in possession of Elizabeth Coleman and William Coleman. (refers to land laid off by order of court to Mary Tucker as her dower). S/ Thomas x Tucker, Wit: John Clay, Wm. Clay, Jesse Clay.

DB 22-405, 29 Oct 1806, rec 1807, Nelson Tucker & Mary Tucker to Archerbald Coleman, for L84.6.2, 19 ac., bo John Clay, the long branch, John Eppes, Joshua Eppes, Waugh. S/ Nelson Tucker, Mary Tucker. Wit: John Allen, Lewis Leath, Thos. Worsham, John Wills.

> *NOTE: This deed did not indicate any relationship of Mary to Nelson, but she appears to be his step-mother and widow of Thomas Tucker Sr.*

SUMMARY OF LAND TRANSACTIONS:

|      |                            | PLUS | MINUS | BAL |
|------|----------------------------|------|-------|-----|
| 1766 | 08 9-44 fr Coleman         | 80   |       | 80  |
| 1768 | DB 9-302 fr Berry          | 3    |       | 83  |
|      | adjustment                 | 1    |       | 84  |
| 1773 | DB 12-44 fr Bevill         | 100  |       | 184 |
| 1773 | DB 12-163 to bro. Henry    |      | 42    | 142 |
| 1787 | fr est of father Matthew Sr| 60   |       | 202 |
| 1801 | est to William Coleman     |      | 18    | 184 |
|      | est to son Nelson          |      | 19    |     |
|      | est to son Thomas Jr       |      | 19.75 |     |
|      | est to son Thomas Jr       |      | 15    |     |
|      | est to son Thomas Jr       |      | 10    | 139 |
|      | est to widow Mary (dower)? |      |       |     |

SUMMARY:

Thomas Tucker b c1739, son of Matthew Tucker Sr (the I) of Prince George & Amelia Counties, d 1800 intestate in Amelia Co., m 1st c1760 Lucy _____, m 2nd 1793 in Amelia Co., Mary Coleman, and had issue by his first wife Lucy:

Nelson Tucker b c1775, m 1799 Rhoda Hood.

(?) Rebeccah Tucker b c1776, m 1792 William Roberts.

Thomas Tucker b c1779, m 1800 Elizabeth Coleman.

(?) Phebe Tucker b c1783, m 1799 Edward Hood.

1. Williams, Kathleen Booth, "Marriages of Amelia County, Va. 1735-1815", 1961

# T0152100 - NELSON TUCKER

## MD RHODA HOOD
## SON OF THOMAS TUCKER
## MD 1ST LUCY ____,
## MD 2ND MARY COLEMAN

AMELIA CO. VA

PERSONAL TAX RECORD

1790 1 Thomas Tucker

1791 2 Thomas Tucker, Nelson Tucker
*(See WB 6-128, 1800, Thomas Tucker.).*

*NOTE: Since Nelson Tucker first appeared as a 16-yr-up tithable in the household of Thomas Tucker in 1791, it appears that Nelson Tucker was b c1775, was age 21 c1796, and was son of Thomas Tucker Sr & 1st wf Lucy.*

LAND TAX RECORD

1800-01 Thomas Tucker Est. 202 ac. 1802-07 Thomas Tucker Est. 184 ac.

MARRIAGES [1]

28 Mar 1792, William Roberts m RebeccTucker. Sur. Thomas Hood. p R-3.

23 Jan 1793, Thomas Tucker m Miny (or Mary) Coleman, Sec. Evan Mitchell.

24 Apr 1799, Nelson Tucker m Rhoda Hood, Sec. Solomon Hood.

28 Dec 1799, Edward Hood m Phoebe Tucker, Sur. Abram Hood, m 2 Jan 1800 by Rev. Walthall Robertson who says Phebe. p H-3.

13 Aug 1800, Thomas Tucker m Elizabeth Coleman, Sec. Martin Chandler, Parent John Jones.

DB 21-154, 20 Mar 1801, rec 22 Oct 1801, Nelson Tucker & wf Rhoda, Edward Hood, & Thomas Tucker, to Wm. Coleman, for

L18, 18 ac. (no significant bounds). S/ Nelson x Tucker, Rhoda x Tucker, Thomas Tucker, Rebecker x Roberots. Wit: Wm. Coleman, Jasper x Kidd, Archer Coleman.

> *NOTE: Why "Rebecker Roberots" would sign this deed instead of Edward Hood is a mystery. It appears that the grantor parties to this deed, e.i. Nelson Tucker, Edward Hood, Thomas Tucker and possibly Rebeccah Roberts were heirs of Thomas Tucker Sr, & they sold a part of his est of 202 ac. - 18 ac. = 184 ac. (See Land Tax Record)*

DB 22-405, 29 Oct 1806, rec 1807, Nelson Tucker & Mary Tucker to Archerbald Coleman, for L84.6.2, 19 ac., bo John Clay, the long branch, John Eppes, Joshua Eppes, Waugh. S/ Nelson Tucker, Mary Tucker. Wit: John Allen, Lewis Leath, Thos. Worsham, John Wills.

> *NOTE: This deed did not indicate the relationship of Mary to Nelson, but she appears to be his step-mother, and widow of his father Thomas Tucker Sr.*

Nelson Tucker, having sold his inheritance, did not appear on the Land Tax Records of Amelia Co., and probably moved to another county or state.

SUMMARY:

Nelson Tucker, son of Thomas Tucker & 1st wf Lucy, b c1775 in Amelia Co., m 1799 in Amelia Co. Rhoda Hood.

1. Williams, Kathleen Booth, "Marriages of Amelia County, Va. 1735-1815", 1961

# T0152200 - THOMAS TUCKER JR

## MD ELIZABETH COLEMAN
## SON OF THOMAS TUCKER SR
### MD 1ST LUCY _____,
### MD 2ND MARY COLEMAN

AMELIA CO., VA.

LAND TAX RECORDS

1795-99   Thomas Tucker Sr 202 ac.
1800-01   Thomas Tucker Est 202 ac.
1802-07   Thomas Tucker Est 184 ac.
1808-10   Thomas Tucker Est 139 1/4 ac.
1811-17   Thomas Tucker Est 98 3/4 ac. adj. Elizabeth Kidd & John Clay.

*NOTE: Since Thomas Tucker was listed as Sr in the Land Tax of 1795-99, he had a son named Thomas Jr, b c1779.*

MARRIAGES [1]

28 Mar 1792, William Roberts m Rebecc Tucker. Sur. Thomas Hood. p R-3.

23 Jan 1793, Thomas Tucker m Miny (or Mary) Coleman, Sec. Evan Mitchell.

24 Apr 1799, Nelson Tucker m Rhoda Hood, Sec. Solomon Hood.

28 Dec 1799, Edward Hood m Phoebe Tucker, Sur. Abram Hood, m 2 Jan 1800 by Rev. Walthall Robertson who says Phebe. p H-3.

13 Aug 1800, Thomas Tucker m Elizabeth Coleman, Sec. Martin Chandler, Parent John Jones.

*NOTE: The marriage in 1793 is the second marriage of Thomas Tucker Sr; the marriage in 1800 is that of Thomas Tucker Jr, as evidenced by the following deeds. Since his father was known as Thomas Sr first in 1795, Thomas Jr was b c1779, age 16 in 1795, and age 21 in 1800 when he married.*

DB 21-154, 20 Mar 1801, rec 22 Oct 1801, Nelson Tucker & wf

Rhoda, Edward Hood, & Thomas Tucker, to Wm. Coleman, for L18, 18 ac. (no significant bounds). S/ Nelson x Tucker, Rhoda x Tucker, Thomas Tucker, Rebecker x Roberots.) Wit: Wm. Coleman, Jasper x Kidd, Archer Coleman.

> *NOTE: Why "Rebecker Roberots" would sign this deed instead of Edward Hood is a mystery. It appears that the grantor parties to this deed, e.i. Nelson Tucker, Edward Hood, Thomas Tucker and possibly Rebeccah Roberts were heirs of Thomas Tucker Sr, & they sold a part of his est of 202 ac. - 18 ac. = 184 ac. (See Land Tax Record)*

DB 22-403, 27 Apr 1807, Thomas Tucker & wf Elizabeth to William Coleman, for L35.14.1, 19 3/4 ac., being a part of the land sd Tucker lives on which was left him by his father Thomas Tucker decd on s.s. of the road, bo Elizabeth Coleman, John Wells, the road. S/ Thomas Tucker, Elizabeth Tucker. Wit: Archer Coleman, John Clay, Archer Bevill, Robert Bevill, Braxton Coleman.

DB 22-414. 26 Jul 1807, rec 26 Aug 1807, Thomas Tucker to John Clay, for L9., 10 ac., being a part of the tract of land formerly belonging to Thomas Tucker decd, now in possession of Mary Tucker, on s.s. of the long branch, bo Kidd. S/ Thomas x Tucker. Wit: Robert Clay, William Clay, Jesse Clay, James H. Mumford.

DB 22-448, 15 Aug 1806, rec 1808, Thomas Tucker to John Eppes, for $91., 15 ac., being a part of the land he now lives on which was left him by his father Thomas Tucker Sen decd, on b.s. of Hood's Road, bo. John Eppes, Mary Tucker's dower line,, former property of Abraham Coleman now in possession of Elizabeth Coleman and William Coleman. (refers to land laid off by order of court to Mary Tucker as her dower). S/ Thomas x Tucker, Wit: John Clay, Wm. Clay, Jesse Clay.

> *Since Thomas Tucker Jr disposed of the land inherited from his father Thomas Tucker Sr, he no longer appeared on the Land Tax Records of Amelia Co., and probably moved to another county or state.*

SUMMARY:

Thomas Tucker Jr, son of Thomas Tucker Sr & 1st wf Lucy, b
c1779 in Amelia Co., m 1800 in Amelia Co. Elizabeth Coleman
whose parent was John Jones. He sold all his inheritance by 1808
and left Amelia Co.

1. Williams, Kathleen Booth, "Marriages of Amelia County, Va.
1735-1815", 1961

# T0153000 - HENRY TUCKER

## MD ELIZABETH MURRY

## SON OF MATTHEW TUCKER SR (I)

AMELIA CO. VA.

LIST OF TITHABLES

| | | |
|---|---|---|
| 1762 | | Henry Tucker listed as 16-yr-up tithable in household of his father Matthew Tucker Sr (I). |
| 1763 | 1 | Henry Tucker |
| 1765 | 1 | Henry Tucker |
| 1767 | 1-25 | Henry Tucker |
| 1769 | 1-25 | Henry Tucker |
| 1770 | 1-25 | Henry Tucker |
| 1782 | 1 | Henry Tucker |
| 1783 | 1 | Henry Tucker |
| 1784 | 1 | Henry Tucker |
| 1786 | 3 | Henry Tucker Sen |
| 1787 | 1 | Henry Tucker |
| 1788 | 1 | Henry Tucker |
| 1789 | 1 | Henry Tucker |
| 1790 | 1 | Henry Tucker |
| 1791 | 1 | Henry Tucker |
| 1791 | 1 | Henry Tucker Jr. |

*NOTE: Henry Tucker was included as a 16-yr-up tithable in the household of his father Matthew Tucker Sr (I) in 1762, but was listed as a separate household beginning in 1763. So he was born ca 1742, age 16 in 1758, and age 21 in 1763. Henry Tucker was listed as Sen. in 1786. In 1791, the personal tax lists included a Henry Tucker household and a Henry Tucker Jr. household. This indicates that Henry Tucker Sr had a son named Henry Tucker Jr b c1770, age 16 in 1786, age 21 in 1791.*

# LAND TAX RECORDS

1782     Henry Tucker 67 ac.
1787     alterations - Henry Tucker 67 d of Matthew Tucker 50
1787     Henry Tucker 117 ac.
1788-94 Henry Tucker 107 ac.
1795 96   Henry Tucker Sr 107 ac.

> *NOTE: The 1787 alteration is confusing. Matthew Tucker Sr. (the I) owned 100 ac. at time of his will, and gave to son Thomas plantation whereon I live, and to son Henry - land in his possession. The intent of the alteration is probably that Matthew Jr (II), as executor, passed 50 ac. to Thomas and 50 ac. to Henry. The 50 ac. is most probably 40 ac., which when added to 25 ac. + 42 ac. purchased = 107 ac.*

DB 9-26, 16 Aug 1766, Peter Coleman Senr. to Henry Tucker, for L8., 25 c., bo. Richard Talley, Thomas Tucker, Matthew Tucker Snr, Francis Tucker Jun. Wit: Thomas Berry, John Hood, Matthew x Tucker. Rec. 25 Sep 1766. S/ Peter (p) Coleman, Mattha (m) Coleman.

DB 12-163 , 2 Nov 1773, Thomas Tucker to Henry Tucker for L20., 42 ac. bo. Peter Coleman, Francis Coleman, Matthew Tucker Sen, Henry Tucker. Wit: Thomas Hood, Henry Hall, John Hood Sen. Rec. 25 Nov 1 73. Wife Lucy relinq. dower. S/ Thomas x Tucker, Lucy x Tucker

WB 3-291 will of Matthew Tucker Sr., wd 3 Mar 1784, *(wp not shown -See WB3-357.)*, names:
dau. Phoebe Tucker - negro Isbell, 5 head cattle, bed & furn., for life then to son Matthew Tucker.
son Thomas Tucker - plantation whereon I now live.
son Henr Tucker - the part of land now in his possession.
Ex: son Matthew Tucker, and Absolom Tucker.
Wit: Absolom Tucker, Joseph Bevill (?), Paschal Tucker. S/ Matthew Tucker.

WB 3-357 Est. I&A, Matthew Tucker, decd, 20 Jun 1785, by Evans Mitchell, Joseph Bevill, John Morgan.

*NOTE: It is assumed Matthew Tucker Sr. died in 1785. The land he willed to his son Henry consisted of either 40 or 50 ac.*

MARRIAGE BONDS [1]

6 Mar 1787, Henry Tucker m Elizabeth Murry, Security Field Tanner.
2 Mar 1793, Henry Tucker m Mary Murry, Sec. Abram Burton. Parent Elizabeth Tucker.

*The marriage in 1787 is most probably the second marriage of Henry Tucker Sr to Elizabeth Murry. The marriage in 1793 is most probably that of Henry Tucker Jr to Mary Murry, who names Elizabeth Tucker as parent. Does this mean that Elizabeth Tucker is mother of Mary Murry, or step-mother of Henry Tucker Jr? If Elizabeth Murry Tucker is parent of Mary Murry Tucker, then Henry Tucker Jr. married his step-mother's daughter by a former marriage. ???*

DB 20-265, 15 Feb 1797, Henry Tucker & wf Elizabeth to William Coleman, for L53.10., 107 ac., bo. William Morgan, John Maccray, William Coleman, Thomas Tucker, sd Tucker's line. Wit: John Eppes, Francis Tucker. Rec. 23 *Feb* 1797. S/ Henry Tucker,
Elizabeth Tucker.

*NOTE: Henry Tucker Sr sold all his lands in Amelia Co. in 1797, and neither he nor his son Henry Tucker Jr again appear on the records of Amelia Co.*

*NOTE: The subject Henry Tucker Sr and Jr are not to be confused with another Henry Tucker Sr & Jr who appeared in Halifax Co. VA, beginning in 1800.*

*That Henry Tucker Jr (c1784-1838)(m Elizabeth Green) was son of Henry Tucker Sr (c1746-1816)(m Nancy (Ann)), who was son of George Tucker Sr (c1710-1784) of Lunenburg Co, who was son of Capt Robert Tucker Sr (c1677-1750) of Prince George & Amelia Counties.*

*(See "Tucker Trails Through Southside Virginia" by B. DeRoy Beale, 1986.)*

171

SUMMARY:

Henry Tucker Sr, son of Matthew Tucker Sr (I), b c1742 in Amelia Co., m probably 1st c1763 m probably 2nd in 1787 in Amelia Co., Elizabeth Murry, and had issue by his 1st wf:

Henry Tucker Jr b c1770 in Amelia Co., m 1793 in Amelia Co. Mary Murry dau of Elizabeth Tucker.

Nothing more is known of the subject Henry Tucker family.

1. Williams, Kathleen Booth, "Marriages of Amelia Co., Virginia, 1735-181'", 1961

# Alphabetical Index

174

176

179

180

182

183

184

185

186

www.ingramcontent.com/pod-product-compliance
Lightning Source LLC
Chambersburg PA
CBHW060849280326
41934CB00007B/981